Hemp

Hemp

A SHORT HISTORY OF THE MOST MISUNDERSTOOD PLANT AND ITS USES AND ABUSES

Mark Bourrie

FIREFLY BOOKS

A FIREFLY BOOK

Published by Firefly Books (U.S.) Inc. 2003

First Printing

Publisher Cataloging-in-Publication Data   (U.S.)
Bourrie, Mark, 1957–
  Hemp : a short history of the most misunderstood plant and its uses and abuses / Mark Bourrie. 1st ed.
[160] p. : ill. ; cm.
Includes index.
Summary: A factual account of hemp and its uses from a historical perspective.
ISBN 1-55297-851-6 (pbk.)
1. Hemp — History. 2. Hemp — Miscellanea. I. Title.
677.12 21   SB255.B67 2003

Published in the United States in 2003 by
Firefly Books (U.S.) Inc.
P.O. Box 1338, Ellicott Station
Buffalo, New York, USA
14205

Published in Canada in 2003 by Key Porter Books Limited.

Electronic formatting: Jean Lightfoot Peters
Design: Peter Maher

Printed and bound in Canada

For Marion

Contents

CHAPTER 1

About Cannabis

PHYTANTHOZA-ICONOGRAPHIA,

Sive

onfpectus

Aliquot millium,

Tam Indigenarum quam Exoticarum, ex quatuor mundi partibus, longâ annorum ferie indefeffoque ftudio,

à

JOANNE GUILIELMO WEINMANNO,

Dicafterii Ratisbonenfis Affeffore & Pharmacopola Seniore collectarum

Plantarum, Arborum, Fruticum, Florum

Fructuum, Fungorum. &c.

Quæ

Nitidiffime æri incifæ & fimul diu delidcratæ ac recens inventa arte, vivis coloribus & iconibus, naturæ æmulâ, æmulâ & reprimentur

Per

BARTHOLOMÆUM SEUTERUM; JOANNEM ELIAM RIDINGERUM ET JOANNEM JACOBUM HAIDIUM

Pictores & Chalcographos Auguftanos,

Quorum

Denominationes, Characteres, Genera, Species & Defcriptiones ex optimis, tam prifcis quam neotericis Auctoribus, ordine ac ferie Alphabetica, cum probatiffimo Ufu Medico, Pharmaceutico, Chirurgico ac Oeconomico, Latino & Germanico Idiomate fincere explicatur

à

D. JOANNE GEORGIO NICOLAO DIETERICO,

Sacræ Cæfareæ ac Regiæ Catholicæ Majeft. Confiliario, Sereniffimi Principis de Furftenberg-Stühingen Medico ordinario ac Reipublicæ Ratisbonenfis Phyfico,

Vol. II. C.D.E.F.

Apud prænominatos Pict. & Chalcogr. Auguftæ venium proftat, quorum fumtibus imprimebatur

RATISBONÆ

HEMP: THE PLANT

Hemp is, arguably, the most controversial of the world's plants, so it should come as no surprise that scientists can't agree on the family to which it belongs and argue over the number of its species. The plant is sometimes placed in the fig or mulberry family *(Moraceae)* or the nettle family *(Urticaceae)*, but it's now usually separated with its useful cousin, the hop plant *(Humulus)*, into a distinct family: *Cannabaceae.*

Most botanists believe there is only one species, *Cannabis sativa*, which, through years of cultivation and careful breeding for various qualities, has been developed into many "races" or "varieties," for better fiber, more oil content, or stronger narcotic properties. Breeding and hybridization for the last quality has been the goal of many enthusiastic clandestine breeders who have, since the 1960s, created strains of the marijuana plant that bear very little obvious relation to hemp grown for fiber. High-grade marijuana plants are short and bushy, with many flower buds, while fiber hemp is tall with one small flower top.

Since marijuana's potency comes from chemicals in its pollen, new strains of the plant have a dozen or more thick flower buds branching off from a short stem, while hemp grows straight and tall, with just one or two tiny flowers. Marijuana resembles hemp about as much as the garden rose resembles its cousin, the strawberry.

All cannabis is native to central Asia, where people have grown it as a fiber crop for thousands of years. But even before its use for rope and cloth was discovered, it was grown as a drug both for religious and recreational use.

If hemp did not have narcotic qualities, it would likely still be grown throughout the temperate world as a cheap alternative to cotton and for its oil-bearing seeds. Hemp thrives on relatively poor soil, has a natural ability to keep weeds at bay, and can mature fast enough that, in some growing areas, two harvests are possible in one season. Compared to other oil crops, it is not as demanding of the land's nutrients as corn and can resist weeds more effectively than canola (rape seed). Compared to other fiber crops, it is easier to grow than flax and is far less labor-intensive, pest-problematic, and climatically finicky than cotton.

But hemp is not just any cash crop, and acceptance of it is a litmus test in Western society. For many anti-drug advocates, especially in the United States, marijuana, even the very weak variety from the hemp fiber plant, is the "gateway drug" to opiates and synthetic narcotics. All ingestible cannabis products containing any tetrahydrocannabinol (THC), the chemical that gives cannabis its drug properties, are banned in the U.S. and Canada, and commercial hemp growing is banned. In other developed countries, marijuana is perceived as a relatively harmless recreational drug and a plant with some interesting industrial and medical applications; hemp agriculture is permitted under government supervision, and new hemp oil and fiber products are being developed quickly.

Hemp activists in the United States would like to see the door opened to the commercial use of an oil seed and fiber plant that used to be grown throughout the Northeast and Midwest. About one-third of Americans, according to recent polls, also want an end to the arrest and jailing of people who use a drug that causes far less misery in the country than alcohol. It is the latter issue that dominates and controls debate on the former.

Take drug hysteria out of the equation, and consider hemp as a crop in competition with other fiber—as *Scientific American* magazine did in 1937, the year hemp was banned, and as many advocates do now—and hemp appears to be a profitable, maybe even lucrative, cash crop. The economic factors—hemp cultivation, harvesting and processing, are very labor-intensive—that conspired against its use for so long are now hemp's assets. In the West, technology has replaced brute labor in the fields. With labor costs now negligible, hemp can be seen as a dollars-per-acre issue. And, taken that way, hemp is competitive. The world doesn't need more sailing ship rope—the main reason hemp was grown in Europe—but the fiber has many other uses, as do the seeds and much of the rest of the plant.

Jute, ramie, abaca, sisal, kenaf, and cotton are fiber crops adapted to hot latitudes. Hemp and flax were the textile crops of temperate regions. In Europe, linen was preferable to hemp, but both can be made into tough, warm, comfortable cloth. Hemp clothing was more popular in Eastern Europe than in France, Britain, and the Low Countries, which were, in their day, the world's center for wool and linen production. Geography and agriculture dictated local custom: Eastern Europeans wore hemp because local people grew it. The cool climate and paid-labor economic system of Western Europe favored flax and wool production. Later, the cotton mills built in the Industrial Revolution turned out cotton cloth, relying on cheap, slave-grown cotton of the U.S. South, and raw materials from India, Egypt, and other tropical regions of the British Empire.

Hemp plant from an 18th-century botany manual.

The local hemp cloth business died out, as did, with the advent of the steamship, the need for most hemp rope. Ironically, hemp was abandoned at a time when plant breeding was taking off. Hemp is very easily bred to produce differing attributes: higher fiber, greater seed count, adaptability to tougher climates. The suppression of hemp agriculture in the 1930s has, until very recently, stopped hemp agricultural experimentation, and many of the original seed strains have been lost or are in danger of extinction. The plant is, however, making a comeback. As an industrial plant, it's being legally grown in Canada, Europe, Asia, and Hawaii. The Sioux of the U.S. West have taken up hemp agriculture and are locked in a fight with the federal government over their right to grow it.

Marijuana strains are more productive and diverse as ever. The United Kingdom, most European countries, and Canada have decided that it's not worth the trouble of prohibiting consumption of cannabis and have taken marijuana possession out of their criminal law or plan to do so soon. In these countries, marijuana possession is treated as an offence similar to a traffic violation (though large-scale growers and dealers are still prosecuted). Only in the United States (and countries depending on its aid, military assistance, and trade) is propaganda against marijuana use given serious credibility. The next decade or two will show whether hemp cultivation will make a comeback in the United States, and if the government will redirect its energy from prosecuting the users of a relatively harmless recreational drug to more serious social problems.

HEMP IN HISTORY

Hemp fibers have been found in Chinese archaeological sites of 4000 B.C. It turns up in Turkestan and Egypt in 3000 B.C. The Greeks and Romans did not grow hemp but imported it from Asia and Gaul. Hemp growing continued in northern Europe after the fall of Rome, although it was never a major crop in the developed world. Hemp was grown in western Russia, Transylvania, and Bulgaria in the Middle Ages and the early Industrial Age; in developing countries in the 20th century.

Hemp farming was hard work; hemp had to be cut by hand and gathered into shocks to dry before being spread on the field for retting (soaking). After retting, the stems were gathered up and broken using a hemp brake. Next the hemp was hackled by flaying it on a pincushion of long needles to further separate the fiber from the inner woody core of the plant, called the "hurd." Hemp farming, especially the separation of fibers in the harvested stalks, was so labor intensive that the feudal estates of Russia, Prussia, and Poland, with their millions of serfs, undercut the tenant farms and wage labor of Western Europe. The collapse of the serf system in the 1860s in Eastern Europe forced the hemp business to find other sources of cheap labor, and the plantations of southeast Asia expanded to meet the demand.

Henry VIII was the first English monarch to go out of his way to encourage the cultivation of hemp for rope fiber, and, as the importance of England's navy (and soon after, France's, Spain's, and Holland's) grew, so did the official sponsorship of hemp growing. People found dozens of uses for hemp and its by-products. For instance, cold hemp tea was used in 17th-century England by anglers to force earthworms out of the ground.

Hemp made a brief comeback during World War II, when the navy needed a domestic supply for rope.

New France and New England were expected to supply the rope for the ships of their colonial masters, although colonial farmers were not always enthusiastic. Landowners could never find enough workers to grow and process hemp, which is much more labor intensive than most food crops. Because of the chronic shortage of laborers in colonial North America, wages were relatively high. So were food prices. In New England, where some towns doubled in size every year between 1630 and 1650, cattle sold for five times the amount that farmers received in England for the same animals. In times of war, speculators drove up the price of food to incredible heights, and naval blockades sometimes cut off supplies from the mother countries. Famine was a real possibility, especially in the young cities. It simply wasn't worth the effort to clear land and pay workers to grow a crop that had such a low profit margin.

Colonial governments alternated between using carrots and sticks to make farmers grow hemp, which was so strategic to navies and trading fleets. Nevertheless, in New France, colonists could make much more money going into the wilderness to trade with the Native peoples for furs. Local administrations strongly discouraged this, through fines, whippings, and jail time, to keep young men on the farms. The government was backed by the Roman Catholic Church, which had succeeded in keeping Protestants out of New France and wanted to create an idyllic feudal state in the St. Lawrence Valley. The unlicensed fur traders, called *coureurs du bois* (bush runners), were denounced as a nasty lot who peddled brandy to the Natives, married Native women, and were lost to the Church.

All of the propaganda had a positive effect on the hemp business. In 1709 — a century after the founding of the colony — the colonial intendent (business manager) Jacques Raudot wrote to Colonial Minister Pontchartrain praising the local farmers for finally getting down to the business of clearing the land and doing something useful for the navy and the balance books of France:

> *It is true, monseigneur, that the colony of Canada, after having cost so much to His Majesty, is of very little use. This situation is attributable to the disorderliness of the inhabitants and the great value of the beaver pelts. The inhabitants of this country are now starting to see the error of their ways. They are cultivating their lands, and making hemp and linens; and if they are encouraged to stay this course, they will ultimately make this country useful to France...; if the iron mines of Trois-Rivières are opened in the future, and if rope and sailcloth are produced in this country, everybody will start building, but only time can have this effect.*

In the late 1600s, the farmers at the manor farm of Platon Ste. Croix, near Quebec City, were among the most enthusiastic hemp growers in the colony. They rented their farms from the Ursuline nuns. The farmers of Acadia, along Canada's Atlantic coast, had been growing hemp since 1606, and kept supplying the French navy until the British expelled them to Louisiana in 1755. One hundred and fifty years later their descendants, the Mississippi Delta "Cajuns," would be among the first Americans to embrace marijuana smoking.

English colonists brought hemp to Virginia in 1611, but, despite the opposition of King James I, neglected the crop for the more profitable local drug, tobacco. The Pilgrim Fathers were busy if reluctant hemp growers, bringing seeds with them to New England in 1628 and establishing large hemp farms outside Salem. Two years later, the first hemp rope work (a processing plant called a ropewalk) was opened in Boston. A second, much larger one, operated by John Harrison, a rope-maker from Salisbury, was built at the foot of Summer Street. It was to become one of the city's most important employers and a focus of discontent that would contribute to the local desire for independence from Great Britain.

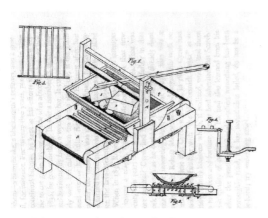

A 19th-century print of a hemp breaker, a machine used to prepare fibers.

Harrison had tremendous political clout in the city. When John Heyman tried to open a competing factory in 1663, the city authorities forced him to leave town and open his factory across the harbor, in Charlestown. Heyman held on to his Boston monopoly for another decade, until his death. Within a few years, Boston had dozens of ropewalks. The demand for hemp was so high that Boston rope-makers had to bring in tons of it from Eastern Europe, via the ports of England and Scotland. As late as 1770, on the eve of the American Revolution, some 400 tons of hemp fiber were imported from the Baltic, through Great Britain, in the first six months of the year because local farmers couldn't, or wouldn't, meet the demand.

After the Revolution freed hemp imports from the control of British firms, American ships traded directly with the Russians and Prussians, and imports into the new United States rose from 3,400 tons in 1800 to nearly 5,000 tons between 1820 and 1840. Each year between 1839 and 1843, the Charlestown Navy yard processed an average of 500 tons of Russian hemp but only seven tons of American-grown hemp. This imbalance of trade alarmed the government, but, because the Navy thought Russian hemp was superior to locally grown fiber and because local farmers didn't really want to grow it, the government's concerns went unheeded.

Ropewalks, some over 700 feet (213 m) long, were huge wooden firetraps, potential neighborhood-destroying bombs loaded with dry fiber and tar. Boston tried to keep them out of the center of the city by locating them on peninsulas, but the city grew around them, often with disastrous results. Just after the Revolution, there were 14 ropewalks in Boston, near Boston Common and along Pearl Street (now the city's financial district). On July 30, 1794, a fire broke out in the ropewalks and flattened much of the neighborhood from Milk Street to Cow Lane (now High Street).

The ropewalks were relocated to the marshy flats along the Charles River at the foot of the Boston Common, where factory owners built a sea wall and reclaimed the tidal flats. After the decline of the hemp rope business, the Back Bay eventually became one of the most fashionable parts of the city, and, after the city bought back the land in 1824, home of the Public Gardens.

Ports are tough places, and rope factories were an integral part of ports. The work was hard, the pay was poor, but ropewalks offered one of the few opportunities for indigent immigrants to make some cash. The competition for the jobs was stiff. So, when poorly paid and unpopular British soldiers stationed in Boston in the winter of 1770 tried to moonlight by applying for part-time jobs in the ropewalks, trouble was inevitable. Local toughs greeted the British soldiers and roughed them up. The soldiers' colleagues returned the nastiness, touching off street violence that escalated into one of the most famous incidents in American history, the Boston Massacre.

On March 2, Patrick Walker, a soldier of the 29th Infantry, went to the huge ropewalk owned by John Grey. Witnesses say foul words were exchanged between the two. Grey asked the soldier, "Will you work?" When the soldier said he would, Grey replied, "Then go and clean my shithouse." Blows were exchanged, and, during the fight, rope-maker Nicholas Ferriter got the better of Walker and disarmed the soldier of his cutlass. Humiliated, the soldier went back to his barracks for help.

A Bostonian picks up the story, describing, in an affidavit taken two weeks after the subsequent "massacre," some of the brawling that led to it:

> I, John Hill, aged sixty-nine, testify, that in the afternoon of Friday the second of March current, I was at a house the corner of a passage way leading from Atkinson's street to Mr. John Gray's rope-walks, near Green's barracks so called, when I saw eight or ten soldiers pass the window with clubs. I immediately got up and went to the door, and found them returning from the rope-walks to the barracks; whence they again very speedily re-appeared, now increased to the number of thirty or forty, armed with clubs and other weapons. In this latter company was a tall Negro drummer, to whom I called, 'you black rascal, what have you to do with white people's quarrels?' He answered, 'I suppose I may look on,' and went forward. I went out

directly and commanded the peace, telling them I was in commission; but they not regarding me, knocked down a rope-maker in my presence, and two or three of them beating him with clubs, I endeavored to relieve him; but on approaching the fellows who were mauling him, one of them with a great club struck at me with such violence, that had I not happily avoided it might have been fatal to me. The party last mentioned rushed in towards the rope-walks, and attacked the rope-makers nigh the tar-kettle, but were soon beat off, drove out of the passage-way by which they entered, and were followed by the rope-makers, whom I persuaded to go back, and they readily obeyed. And further I say not.

The soldiers sulked for a while in their barracks, then rounded up an even larger force. This time 40 soldiers, armed with clubs and acting without the permission of their officers, took another run at the ropeworkers. A local justice of the peace was able to break up the melee, but fighting between small groups of off-duty soldiers and rope-makers continued for another couple of days. The commander of the soldiers, Lieutenant Colonel Maurice Carr, tried to stop the disorder, asking the lieutenant governor to somehow persuade the young men of Boston to stop brawling with his soldiers (who, by all accounts, still seemed to be getting the worst of these fights). On the evening of March 4, 1770, a sergeant did not answer roll call, and a rumor spread among the soldiers that he had been murdered. Carr decided to send his men to search the ropewalks. The sergeant turned up alive and well in a tavern, but events were now out of control.

The next day, Sunday, the ropewalks were closed. A mob of young men and teenage boys wandered the downtown streets and beat up any soldiers they could find. The next day, a mob formed outside the Customs House. Local radicals joined the rope-makers and worked to turn the trouble into a political issue.

On the night of March 5, Captain Thomas Preston led a squad of soldiers from their barracks. The soldiers were looking for trouble, yelling into the crowd, "Where are the damned boogers, cowards, where are your Liberty Boys?" They marched toward the Customs House, the center of tax collection in the city. Bells ringing in the fire halls alerted people across the city that there was trouble. The mob grew larger. Men with sticks hurled insults at the soldiers; boys threw snowballs. Captain Preston tried to restrain his men, but, as tension built, one soldier fired his gun into the crowd. The rest of the line of troops followed. Three people in the mob were dead, two others would die in the next few days, and five others were wounded.

The soldiers were ably defended by John Adams, one of the leading radicals in the city. He would go on to become the United States' second president. Two of the soldiers were convicted of manslaughter and were punished by having the letter "M" branded into their thumbs. What should have been a local fight over jobs became a symbol of the struggle between colonists and the foreign authorities. Boston seethed for five years before open warfare broke out and the hills around the city became armed camps and battlefields.

Of course, war was always good for the hemp business, and the ropewalks of Boston and Charleston, along with their counterparts in Britain, France, and Spain, were kept busy supplying the rigging for the fleets that fought the naval battles and supplies to the armies of Washington, Howe, Burgoyne, and Cornwallis.

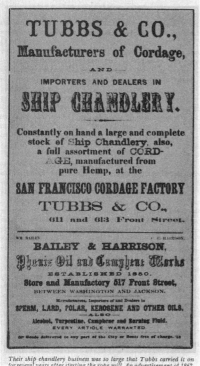

Before the Reefer Madness scares of the 1930s, hemp was a valued crop used mostly for ships' rigging.

For a time following the War of Independence, farmers could pay their taxes in hemp. George Washington admonished, "Sow it everywhere." Thomas Jefferson, a strong proponent of hemp as a crop, invented a hemp brake and experimented with different genetic varieties.

In 1837 a steam-powered rope-making complex was completed at the Charlestown Navy yard that manufactured most of the U.S. Navy's cordage until the complex closed in 1971. Designed by Alexander Parris, better known as the architect of Boston's Quincy Market, this historic facility includes a tar house, a hemp house, and America's only remaining full-length ropewalk, a stone structure stretching one-quarter of a mile (.4 km) long. Even during the Navy yard's tough times in the 1880s, the ropewalk provided constant work. The nascent equal rights movement benefited during both world wars when women were employed as rope-makers. When the U.S.S. *Constitution* was virtually rebuilt from 1927 to 1931, the ropewalk manufactured the ancient-style, four-stranded hemp, shroud-laid cordage required for her standing rigging.

Charlestown's ropewalk is now slated for restoration, and tall ships may once again be rigged with hempen cordage from this monument, which literally and figuratively lies in the shadow of Bunker Hill and *Old Ironsides*.

After American settlers crossed the Appalachians, hemp farming centered in the marginal farm country of Kentucky, which turned out baling rope and bagging used for cotton bales. Hemp accounted for 5 percent of the weight of a cotton bale, and the fortunes of the Kentucky industry rose and fell with the cotton market. The Kentucky farmers could have grown much more if the U.S. Navy had bought their product, but the Navy continued using imported Russian "Riga Rein" hemp, which, the old salts claimed, was better. It was water-retted (soaking hemp thoroughly in large ponds), a process that U.S. farmers resisted because of its high labor cost.

In 1841, the U.S. government, in an attempt to end the drain of government cash to Russian and Prussian hemp farmers, tried to kick-start the country's hemp industry by paying a bounty of US $280 per ton for American water-retted hemp, provided it was suitable for naval cordage. Many farmers prepared large pools to water-ret the hemp they produced, using slaves to do the work. But many slaves died of pneumonia, malaria, and cholera contracted from working in the hemp pools, and the practice was abandoned.

The Civil War was a watershed for the hemp industry. The first ironclad steam-driven warships were launched during the war, foretelling the end of sail. Although another 80 years would pass before the last sailing ships left the seas, there were other threats to the hemp industry: just before the Civil War, the first abaca rope came on the market. Abaca, a relative of the banana,

SIEGE OF
LEXINGTON, MO.
SEPT 18, 19, 20, 1861.

Confederates won the siege of Lexington, Montana, by using hemp bales as fortifications.

became popular because it floated, did not require tarring, and could be produced with cheap labor on plantations in the East Indies.

Hemp had a role in a land battle, albeit a fairly minor one. In 1863, the Confederate Missouri State Guard, which controlled most of the state, attacked Union forces in Lexington. Confederate Major General Sterling Price tried to drive the 3,500 Union soldiers from their trenches, but couldn't make headway against his enemies' cannon and musket fire. After two days of fighting, Price ordered his men to make movable breastworks from hemp bales from the town's ropeworks. The Confederates, hiding behind this effective shielding, were able to reach and break through the Union lines. Once the rebels had broken the Union line, the federal commander asked for terms of surrender, and, two hours later, his men laid down their weapons.

The battlefield is now a historic site, but Civil War re-enactors, who work so hard to make their hobby authentic, can't get real hemp bales for their shows. Because Kentucky stayed loyal to the Union, the Lincoln government looked for ways to help its hemp farmers. The government helped set up cloth mills to supply cloth for the war effort and paid top prices for Kentucky hemp for the now less-finicky Navy. After the war, however, the industry fell into a steep decline.

Harvesting American Hemp, I H C Farm, Grand Forks, N. D.

AMERICAN HEMP
A New Crop and a Weed Fighter
1. A tall growing annual plant that produces fibre suitable for binder twine, rope, carpet and linen.

In the early 20th century, the U.S. government encouraged farmers to plant hemp.

The parts of the state that grew hemp became backwaters, relying on the cheap labor of former slaves who worked the winter months breaking hemp. The ready availability of this labor force, and its dependence on hemp processing for subsistence, became one reason Kentucky's hemp industry's transition to mechanization in the early 20th century was delayed. Post–Civil War freer trade with countries that exported cheap tropical fibers killed off even more hemp operations, jute and iron bands replaced hemp for cotton bales, and Kentucky farmers sought other valuable crops.

After the Civil War, hemp farms started in Minnesota, which had an influx of settlers from hemp-growing regions of Eastern Europe and Scandinavia, but the acreages stayed small. Hemp competed with jute and sisal for a piece of the binder twine market, but for two generations, the future seemed bleak. Economics continually worked against the spread of the crop in America.

However, in 1917, German inventor George Schlichten created a decorticator to allow industrial-scale processing of hemp pulp for competitive paper making. Finally, it seemed, someone had solved the labor problem that had, since the beginning of agriculture, dogged hemp.

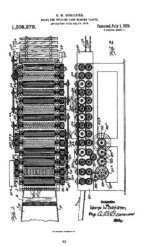

1,308,378.

93

In 1919 inventor George Schlichten patented a new machine that would have made hemp profitable.

The February 1937 issue of *Popular Mechanics* announced a new wonder crop. Hard-pressed American farmers, now into the ninth year of the Great Depression, were promised an annual windfall of

...several hundred million dollars, all because a machine has been invented which solves a problem more than 6,000 years old. It is hemp, a crop that will not compete with other American products. Instead, it will displace imports of raw material and manufactured products produced by underpaid coolie and peasant labor and it will provide thousands of jobs for American workers throughout the land.

The machine which makes this possible is designed for removing the fiber-bearing cortex from the rest of the stalk, making hemp fiber available for use without a prohibitive amount of human labor.

Hemp is the standard fiber of the world. It has great tensile strength and durability. It is used to produce more than 5,000 textile products, ranging from rope to fine laces, and the woody "hurds" remaining after the fiber has been removed contain more than seventy-seven per cent cellulose, and can be used to produce more than 25,000 products, ranging from dynamite to Cellophane.

Machines now in service in Texas, Illinois, Minnesota and other states are producing fiber at a manufacturing cost of half a cent a pound, and are finding a profitable market for the rest of the stalk. Machine operators are making a good profit in competition with coolie-produced foreign fiber while paying farmers fifteen dollars a ton for hemp as it comes from the field.

The machine was comparable to the cotton gin, which had revived the cotton industry in the Deep South a century before.

Hemp could be grown anywhere in the United States, the article noted, and could be planted after other crops had been taken in. Hemp was just the crop to save the American countryside from the economic misery caused by the pathetic prices that were being paid for corn, wheat, and livestock, which had not been as low since the time of Shakespeare.

The magazine reported that

under old methods, hemp was cut and allowed to lie in the fields for weeks until it "retted" enough so the fibers could be pulled off by hand. Retting is simply rotting as a result of dew, rain and bacterial action. Machines were developed to separate the fibers mechanically after retting was complete, but the cost was high, the loss of fiber great, and the quality of fiber comparatively low.

With the new machine, known as a decorticator, hemp is cut with a slightly modified grain binder. It is delivered to the machine where an automatic chain conveyor feeds it to the breaking arms at the rate of two or three tons per hour. The hurds are broken into fine pieces that drop into the hopper, from where they are delivered by blower to a baler or to truck or freight car for loose shipment. The fiber comes from the other end of the machine, ready for baling.

From this point on almost anything can happen. The raw fiber can be used to produce strong twine or rope, woven into burlap, used for carpet warp or linoleum backing or it may be bleached and refined, with resinous by-products of high commercial value. It can, in fact, be used to replace the foreign fibers which now flood our markets.

Popular Mechanics noted that an American munitions maker was already using thousands of tons of hemp hurds to manufacture dynamite and TNT. A large paper company, which had been paying more than a million dollars a year in duties on foreign-made cigarette papers, had switched to hemp grown in Minnesota.

And the magazine downplayed the connection with marijuana:

[T]he blossom of the female hemp plant contains marijuana, a narcotic, and it is impossible to grow hemp without producing the blossom. Federal regulations now being drawn up require registration of hemp growers, and tentative proposals for preventing narcotic production are rather stringent. However, the connection of hemp as a crop and marijuana seems to be exaggerated. The drug is usually produced from wild hemp or locoweed which can be found on vacant lots and along railroad tracks in every state. If federal regulations can be drawn to protect the public without preventing the legitimate culture of hemp, this new crop can add immeasurably to American agriculture and industry.

It was too late. While the magazine was on the presses, the U.S. government had passed the *Marijuana Tax Act* and dealt the industry its death blow.

REEFER MADNESS

As the hemp rope industry was declining, a much older use for cannabis engaged the public's attention. Marijuana, a fringe drug in Western Europe and North America, suddenly became popular, probably because of one invention: the rolling paper.

Marijuana smoking may be older than agriculture: 15,000-year-old bone pipes were found at the Non Nak Tha archaeological site in Thailand. Some 10,000 years later, the Chinese began cultivating hemp for fiber. Chinese doctors learned of its pharmaceutical uses, and, by 220 B.C., the physician Hao-tho recommended surgeons mix it with wine as an anesthetic: "After a certain number of days or the end of a month the patient finds he has recovered without having experienced the slightest pain during the operation," Hao-tho wrote.

By 1000 B.C., cannabis, along with opium, was used throughout India. *The Zend-Avesta*, written in 600 B.C., sings the praises of its intoxicating resin. Its use spread slowly; it took nearly 2000 years for cannabis to spread through the subcontinent, and, during much of that time, it was simply part of the pharmaceutical inventory of physicians. Just before the Muslim invasion of northern India in the 10th century, Indians began smoking cannabis as a recreational drug, mainly as a spiritual exercise.

The effects of cannabis, even more than other hallucinogens, are highly variable from person to person and from one plant strain to another. The recent underground development of extremely strong strains of cannabis has increased this variability. Something similar has happened with

A parade of beautiful but ruined women graced the covers of anti-marijuana novels in the 1930s.

coca: the coca leaves chewed by Incas of the Peruvian Andes deaden hunger and ward off boredom, while refined cocaine gives a much stronger high with abrupt and profound (though temporary) psychological changes. The lowest-THC marijuana, "ditch weed," smoked in Mexico, and, until the late 1930s, growing wild throughout most of the United States, contains so little THC that smokers relied on a combination of hyperventilation, anticipation, and volume to get high. Only in Asia did people make marijuana resins into hashish and other strong concentrates, with less social damage than that caused by imperialism, alcohol, or opiates pushed on them by foreign governments.

Being fairly easy to breed and change, marijuana's constituents can be unstable. Over a period of time, usually about six hours, for example, the inactive cannabidiolic acid converts to active tetrahydrocannabinols and eventually to inactive cannabinol. These chemical changes usually take place more rapidly in tropical climates. Plants of different ages or from different regions may thus vary in narcotic effect. And, because of selective breeding, most of the marijuana grown today is far stronger than the plants grown in the 1960s, when marijuana smoking became part of mass culture.

For most people, marijuana's principal effect is euphoria: gentle, confident well-being, sometimes punctuated by "rushes" of rather pleasant feelings, including a greater appreciation of ideas and art. True hallucinations are fairly rare and are mild. Some regular users find marijuana makes them feel tired or anxious, and tend to stop smoking it. It's not a good recreational drug for people with panic disorder, depression, or who are dealing with grief and mourning. However, for most users, cannabis is a drug that makes them feel happy, has a much less depressive effect than alcohol, and is much less likely than alcohol to bring out latent violence. While alcohol is a factor in many murders and nearly all manslaughter convictions, it's extremely rare for people accused of murder to argue that marijuana use was a contributing factor to their crime. In short, for the vast majority of users, cannabis smoking makes them mellow.

Chinese society was the first culture to try to stamp out cannabis use. In 600 B.C., the emperors of the Chou dynasty commissioned inscriptions mocking cannabis and its users. The ancient Chinese character for cannabis, *Ma*, has a negative connotation, one that suggests the stupefying properties of the drug. Cannabis was, however, the drug of choice for shamans in several parts of China. In 500 B.C., a Taoist priest who opposed local shamans wrote that cannabis was used by "necromancers, in combination with ginseng, to set forward time and future events." Shamanism declined in the next 2,000 years

An Indian Buddhist monk looks over his hemp crop.

before the opening of direct trade between China and Europe in the 16th century. Hemp was still grown for fiber, but China seems to have forgotten the plant's use as a drug. The next smoking drug to spread through China was opium, thrust on the country by foreign governments to extract gold, tea, and porcelain from the country.

The Scythians, a nomadic people of the southern Russian steppe, introduced cannabis smoking to Europeans. The well-traveled Greek historian and geographer Herodotus, who visited Scythian communities near the Black Sea, had an interesting time among these "barbarians," who had a strong hunger for cannabis. When he got back to Greece, Herodotus described a sort of marijuana sauna used by the Scythians:

They have a sort of hemp growing in this country, very like flax, except in thickness and height. In this respect the hemp is far superior: it grows both spontaneously and from cultivation... They make a booth by fixing in the ground three sticks inclined toward each other, and stretching around them some woolen pelts which they arrange to fit as close as possible, the Scythians take some seed of this hemp, they creep under the cloths and then put the seed on the red hot stones, immediately it smokes, and produces such a steam, that no Grecian vapor bath would surpass it. The Scythians, transported by the vapor, shout aloud.

Sometimes, he says, the Scythians didn't go to the trouble of building a sweat lodge. They just built a fire and tossed handfuls of hemp flowers into it, then sat downwind. Archaeologists have found ample proof that the Scythians, a creative and prosperous people who have left behind a wealth of artwork and gold jewelry in their frozen tombs in Siberia, were busy cannabis users. Tripods, braziers, charcoal, and pelts with the remains of cannabis resins and leaves have been found in the tombs.

Scythians were swept away around the time of Christ by the

Huns, Goths, and other waves of nasty migrants who spread westward toward the Roman Empire after the construction of the Great Wall of China. The invaders were alcohol users who made strong drink from honey and berries. Disdainful of farming and usually on the move, they didn't have much use for cannabis, but their descendents in Europe would later grow hemp for rope.

The Romans knew about cannabis use in the eastern fringes of their empire and in Persia. Pliny the Elder, a Roman scientist, left us a secondhand description of the use of a plant, probably cannabis, he found in the (now lost) writings of the scholar Democratus:

Taken in drink, it produces a delirium, which presents to the fancy visions of a most extraordinary nature. The angelis, he says, grows upon Mt. Libanus in Syria, upon the chain of mountains called Dicte in Crete, and at Babylon and Susa in Persia. An infusion of it imparts powers of divination to the Magi. The gelotophyllis too, is a plant found in Bactriana, and on the banks of the Borysthenes. Taken internally with myrrh and wine, all sorts of visionary forms present themselves, exciting the most immoderate laughter.

The Romans, while always eager to take up interesting foreign practices, never adopted cannabis. It wasn't a question of morality; no one had developed a relatively easy or enjoyable way of ingesting the flower of the hemp plant. The Scythian smoke houses were extremely wasteful, so the only efficient way to get cannabis into the body was by eating it. The Romans already had a drug-food of choice: alcohol. Wine was one of the cheapest commodities of the Roman Empire, which straddled the great vine-growing regions of the Rhône, the Rhine Valley, Italy, Spain, and Greece. Romans drank wine at all of their meals and it flowed freely at every celebration. Wine production was controlled by lucrative state monopolies, and, like all food in the Empire, was inexpensive because the government subsidized it. Wine was considered a necessity of life, and any shortage was considered catastrophic.

After the barbarian invasions of Europe, cannabis use was, for about 500 years, confined to Persia and the area south of the Hindu Kush. Cannabis was — and still is — used in three different preparations in India. *Bhang,* comparable in potency to marijuana in the United States, is made from the leaves and stems of uncultivated plants and blended into a pleasant-tasting liquid. Poorer Indians use it as a sort of strong beer. *Ganja,* more potent than *bhang,* is made from the tops of cultivated plants, and the use of that word in Jamaica suggests the spread of marijuana from India to the Caribbean through the semi-forced migration of indentured Indian workers in the British Empire. The third and most potent preparation, *charas,* is a form of hashish made by scraping the resin from the flowers and leaves of cultivated plants and pressing it into hard blocks. High-caste Hindus are not permitted to use alcohol, but they are allowed *bhang* at religious ceremonies, weddings, and family gatherings.

Cannabis would come into its own in Islamic countries. Islam spread through the major hemp-growing regions of southwest Asia in the 11th century, at about the same time the smoking pipe become popular. The pipe, seemingly coincidently, was invented in two places at the same time. Hashish pipes were likely developed in northern India and spread northwestward into what's now Pakistan, Iran, and the Middle East. In parts of the Islamic world, hashish smoking was encouraged as an alternative to the use of alcohol. In North America, native peoples developed pipes to smoke tobacco and other plants. In both regions, smoking-pipes started out as simple tubes, then evolved into more elaborate and efficient devices.

A corruption of the word *Ashashin,* combined with a slur against an Islamic movement, hashish has a dubious history, one that has been twisted in the West to darken the reputation of the drug. The Assassin movement, a 12th-century sect, used selective killings to advance the political careers of its leaders. The link between hashish and the Assassins is rather weak, one of linguistics rather than cause and effect. The Assassins called themselves the "New Message." Founded by Prince al-Hasan ibn-al-Sabbah (died 1124), who claimed descent from the Himyarite kings of South Arabia, the movement was headquartered in the mountain fortress of Alamut, 10,200 feet up in the mountains of northern Persia. The fortress overlooked one of the most important trade routes in the country, the road between the Caspian Sea and the great plain of Central Persia. How al-Sabbah took control of the fortress and why he left mainstream Islam to start his new branch of that religion are still mysteries. However, once he started tapping into the trade route, al-Sabbah was able to attract followers, buy weaponry, and spread his influence across the region.

The followers of the New Message were committed to spread a kind of Islam that promised to free adherents from Islamic laws that limited personal freedom. The New Message movement was organized as an army, with unquestioning loyalty to al-Sabbah demanded from all of its followers. Western tradition remembers al-Sabbah as the Old Man of the Mountain, an archfiend who lurked in his fortress while his followers slipped through the dark to kill his Islamic and Crusader enemies with cunning thrusts of the dagger.

Marco Polo erroneously linked al-Sabbah's religious sect and the hashish that was produced throughout Persia, Mesopotamia, and Syria. Polo traveled through the region years after al-Sabbah's death, when his enemies were working hard to blacken his name. *Ashashin* was the Syrian word for both "hashish" and for "fool." (The Syrians were enemies of the Ashashin.) In Marco Polo's accounts, based on stories spread by al-Sabbah's Syrian enemies, al-Sabbah ran a non-stop orgy in those Persian mountains, giving new recruits potions that cast them into a deep sleep, then placing them in a wonderful garden filled with willing women. Adherents, said Polo, believed they had awakened in paradise. Since al-Sabbah controlled this entrance to paradise, his followers need not worry about being killed or caught. Whether Polo heard these stories from the Syrians along the caravan routes or simply rewrote old accounts by the Crusaders, who were fighting in Palestine at the same time as al-Sabbah was building his empire farther east, is still a matter of debate. Polo adds to the error by confusing al-Sabbah with his convert Rashid-al-din Sinan, whose Syrian followers terrorized the Crusaders.

Whether al-Sabbah's recruiting methods were fact or fantasy, there's no doubt he was able to organize a group of selective killers who spread terror through the elites of the Islamic world. In 1092, they killed the illustrious vizier of the Saljug sultanate, Nizam-al-Mulk. Later that year, when the Saljug Sultan Malikshah tried to take revenge by capturing al-Sabbah's fortress, New Message soldiers scattered his armies in a night battle.

After that coup, skillful politicking, selective use of murder, and eloquent proselytizing helped al-Sabbah spread his power through a wide swath of the Middle East and Southwest Asia. The movement survived unchecked until 1256, some 32 years after the death of its founder, when the Mongols seized his fortress on their march into Persia and the Euphrates Valley. Within five years, the New Message was driven from Syria, but it still lives on as a small Islamic sect with members in isolated pockets of Syria, Iran, Oman, Zanzibar, and Pakistan. They are followers of the Aga Khan of Bombay, who is a descendent of the last grand master of Alamut.

Throughout Islamic history, Muslims have had mixed views about cannabis use. The Saudi Arabia–based Wahhabi sect forbids all smoking, while Sunnis and Shiites in North Africa, Iraq, Lebanon, Syria, and Pakistan accept it or, at least, tolerate it. All Muslims, however, consider excessive use and dependence as signs of emotional problems.

Europeans have always associated cannabis use with unfriendly or threatening foreign cultures. Napoleon's colonial administrators in Egypt managed to put the local hashish industry out of business, only to find that it had been quickly taken over by Greek smugglers who imported cannabis from the Ottoman Empire.

The team of 200 scientists attached to Napoleon's invasion of Egypt spent quite a lot of time studying hashish and its effects. The defeat of the French forces sent these scholars hurrying back to Europe to publish books and display collections. Soon, everything Egyptian came into vogue, including the smoking of hashish. Opium smoking was already popular in bohemian circles, but hashish was considered more exotic and less dangerous. The French literary elite—Gautier, Baudelaire, Dumas, Balzac—picked it up, and some of their young readers carried banners demanding the legalization of hashish during the Paris street fighting that toppled the monarchy in 1848.

From the salons of Paris, the stylish use of hashish spread to America. Although opium had been imported into the country for years, the Romantic writers who shied away from the nasty addictiveness of opium embraced hashish as a safe, exhilarating drug that opened new areas of creativity.

Cannabis was considered an exotic drug that was often written about in this great age of travel writing, when steam-driven ocean liners made the world a much smaller place.

A travel writer touring the Middle East on assignment with the *New York Herald* wrote this description of a Syrian hashish party. It ran in the Friday, March 15, 1895, edition:

ORGIES OF THE HEMP EATERS.

Hashish Dreamers' Festival in Northwestern Syria Occurs at the Time of the Full Moon.

WOMEN JOIN THE CEREMONY.

Scenes at the Sacred Dance That Surpass the Wildest Ecstasy of
Any Opium Dream.

THE DRUG AND ITS EFFECTS.

Standing in the outskirts of the little town of Latakieh, in
Northwestern Syria, famous everywhere for the excellent tobacco
which takes its name from the otherwise obscure and insignificant
place—and turning his back on the ramshackle houses, the flea
infested caravansary, the malodorous bazaar and garbage strewn
streets, where the scavenger dogs lie stretched out [in the] noonday
sun—the traveller sees in the distance, beyond a wide stretch of green
slope and alternate level, a low range of hills, on which a soft purple
haze [!] seems always to linger. These hills lie between the Lebanon,
where the fierce Druses dwell in their highland fastnesses, and the
Nahr-el-kebir, "The Mighty River." They are known nowadays as
the Nosairie Mountains, the home of the so-called Nosairiyeh tribesmen, the modern "Assassins," or "Hemp Eaters," as they should be
designated from their ceremonial use of hemp, in Arabic "hashish."

AT THE TIME OF THE FULL MOON.

The festival or gathering of the hemp eaters is celebrated monthly, at
the time of the full moon, the moon being then supposed to exert a
specific influence upon human beings. The sectaries meet under a
sacred oak tree growing upon a hill, about equidistant from Latakieh
and the valley of the Orontes, and close to a tiny village inhabited by
some twenty families of the tribe. There is an enormous drum, some
three feet in diameter, standing at the entrance to the village, a couple
of hundred yards off, and as soon as it begins to darken and the
westering sun appears to have fairly sunk in the waters of the
Mediterranean, which is clearly visible from the elevated hilltop on
which the Nosarriyeh are gathered, a deafening boom comes from the
instrument and rolls over the mountain tops like the rumble of thun-
der, rousing the tribesmen to activity, and in a moment they are on

the alert. Lamps are quickly lit and suspended to the branches of the sacred oak among the dangling rags and buttons and feathers and metal scraps that decorate it. A square heap of wood is built up in front of the tree about a dozen yards from it. A sheep is brought forward by one of the men, and the rest of the tribesmen then gather around, the lamps throwing a dim light on their picturesque figures and grim countenances. The Sheikh puts his hand gently on the head of the bleating animal, it is thrown down, its throat cut, after the fashion of the Moslems, and in little more time than it takes to write the words the fleece is off, the carcass is divided and placed on the wood heap, to which fire is applied and kept up till all flesh as well as timber is utterly consumed. Now the Nosarriyeh seat themselves in a circle upon the earth, the Shiekh in the centre, with an attendant on either hand, one holding a large earthenware bowl containing a liquid, the other a bundle of stems to which leaves are attached — the leaves of the sacred hemp plant. The chief takes the stems in his left and the bowl in his right hand and slowly walks around the circle, stopping in front of each man present, who takes from him, first the greenery, at which he sniffs gently, then the bowl, the contents of which he sips. The vessel contains a sweetened infusion of hemp, strong and subtle in its action.

WHAT THE DECOCTION IS LIKE.

The taste of the decoction is sweet, nauseously so, not unlike some preparations of chloroform, and its first effects are anything but pleasant, for it produces a distinct tendency to vomit, not unlike a strong dose of ipecacuahna. As soon as all have in succession partaken of the drink, which is termed "homa", big horns are produced containing spirits, for the Nosarriyeh are great dram drinkers. The horns of liquor are passed about and in a few moments the effects are apparent, following upon the hemp. The eyes brighten, the pulse quickens, the blood seems to bound more actively in the veins, and a restlessness takes possession of the whole body. At this moment the booming of a giant drum is heard again, giving the signal for the sacred dance which is the next item in the ceremonial of the evening. From each of the dozen parties or so into which the clansmen are divided one steps out, and the dozen individuals so designated form up against a gentle declivity in rear of them. Two of the tribe with a "reba," one string fiddle, and a tambourine, seat themselves and start a peculiar air in a minor key, which all those around take up, clapping their hands the while rhythmically, and to this rhythm the dancers, joining hands as they stand, begin to move gently to and fro. The moonlight is full on them, showing up their white nether garments, but leaving the dusky faces and dark upper garments in a semi-shadow. First the dancers move slowly, a few steps to the right and further to the left they go each time, till the movement becomes a positive allegro. Faster goes the music, faster the dancers, until with a finale furioso the men stop, panting and out of breath, at the signal of the Sheikh. He claps his hands and twelve others step out, and the figure begins as before. When these are exhausted a fresh set take their place, and this is continued until each of the clansmen has taken part in the dance. In conclusion all join hands and go seven times round the sacred oak in the direction left to right.

A CRAZY FESTIVAL.

The solemn supper is now ready, and is served by the wives of the tribesmen, who have been busy preparing it in huge earthenware dishes placed upon the ground in the middle of each group. And the moonlight meal in the shade of the sacred oak is none the less striking by reason of its being dished up by women who wear in their shash-bands a sharp yataghan, of which the handle shows clearly, and a brace of pistols in the girdle. The plates are peculiar. First there is fried liver, eaten to the accompaniment of fiery arrack—the favorite spirit of the hemp eaters. Then comes "leben"—a species of sour cooked cream, with more "arak;" afterward the "kibabs" of mutton, in slices on little wooded sticks, like the familiar ware of the cat's meat man; eggs filled with a force meat of rice, tomato, mutton and onions and "pillau." Each person has a wooden spoon to eat with, and the etiquette of the table requires one to eat much and eat quickly, and to drink as much as one eats. The appetites of the Nosairiyeh are proverbial in Syria, the usual allowance of meat being a sheep or two. I can vouch for their tippling powers. Scores of them finish their pint horn of arrack in a couple of draughts, taking a couple of quarts in the course of their supper. The meal is really a match against time, and, with such good trencher men as the hemp eaters, is quickly finished. The real business of the evening now begins. The hemp, powdered and mixed with sirup, is brought round in bowls, together with the decoction of the leaves well sweetened. Each of the tribesmen secures a vessel of arrack—for it quickens and heightens the action of the drugs—and disposes himself in the most comfortable attitude he can think of. Then, taking a good spoonful of the hemp, and washing it down with an equally good drink from the liquor receptacle, he lies or leans back to allow it to operate. I take a reasonable allowance of the compound (it tastes very much like raw tea leaves flavored with sugar water), and then lie back to note the action on my own person, and watch, so far as I can, its effects upon the modern assassins whose systems are seasoned and more accustomed to the drug. Five, ten minutes pass, and there is no sensation; the men around me, with closed eyes, look like waxwork figures. Another ten minutes, and the pulse begins to beat rapidly, the heart commences to thump against the sides of the chest, the blood seems to rush to the head, and there is a sensation of fullness, as if the skull would be burst asunder at the base. There is a roaring in the ears, and strange lights, blurred and indistinct, pass before the eyes. In a moment and quite suddenly all of this passes off, leaving a feeling of delicious languor, and an idea that one is rising from the ground and floating in space. Little things assume an enormous size, and things seem far off.

EFFECTS OF THE DRUG.

The oak tree close by appears to be a mile off, and the cup of drink looks a yard across, the size of a big barrel. One's hands and feet feel heavy and cumbersome, and then feel as if they were dropping off, leav-

ing one free to soar away from the earth skyward, where the clouds seem to open to receive one, and one long perspective of light shines before the eyes. The feeling is one of estactic [sic] restfulness, contented unconsciousness, suggesting the "ninirvana" [sic] of the Buddhist. This marks always the end of the first stage of hemp eating. The aphrodisiac effects, the visions of fair faces and beauteous forms, the voluptuous dreams and languishing fancies which the Easterns experience—these are the results of larger and oft repeated doses of the drug.

Already the larger quantities of the compound, repeated many times in the meantime and stimulated by frequent draughts of arrack, are beginning to show their results upon the hitherto immobile figures of the Nosiariyeh round the sacred oak. Again and again they seize the spoon and convey it to their mouths, until the hemp craze is fully upon them. One or two stir uneasily; then another screams for "Ali, Ali!" (their founder Ali), who is identical, they say with Allah. A half a dozen respond lustily, "Ali hu Allah!" then empty the arrack cups beside them.

A few move about with outstretched arms as though they were in the clouds trying to clutch the houris, whose imaginary forms they see, and disappointed, sink back, after a fresh supply of the drug has been swallowed. From the extremity beyond, where the women are located, come the sound of singing and of laughter and the rhythmic patter of feet upon the ground. The ladies have been indulging on their own account, and the noise they make rouses the men from their dreams. Three or four jump up from the floor at a single bound, and, seized by the dance mania, begin capering away as for very life. They jig here and there, they twine and twist, and writhe and wriggle and distort themselves, awakening [fragment missing] blows off his matchlock as he capers merrily round, while his neighbor stretches out his fingers for the arrack.

Closer to home, in 1854, travel writer Bayard Taylor wrote in the *Atlantic Monthly* of his fun with hashish:

The sense of limitation—of the confinement of our senses within the bounds of our own flesh and blood—instantly fell away. The walls of my frame were burst outward and tumbled into ruin, and without thinking what form I wore—losing sight even of all idea of form—I felt that I existed throughout a vast extent of space... the spirit (demon shall I rather say) of hasheesh [sic] had entire possession of me. I was cast upon the flood of his illusions, and drifted helplessly withersoever they might choose to bear me. The thrills which ran through my nervous system became more rapid and fierce, accompanied with sensations that steeped my whole being in unutterable rapture.

Taylor, in describing his hashish rushes, was one of the first Americans to put his THC experience in writing, but, of course, was not the last.

But war, rather than the experimentations of Romantic writers, determines how American and European cultures view drugs. Just seven years after Taylor wrote about his hash smoking, his country was mired in one of history's most destructive civil wars. War came at a time when opiates were the only effective painkillers for the vicious wounds that soldiers faced from large-caliber, slow-moving musket balls, grapeshot, cannon balls, bayonets, and cavalry sabers. Many men wracked with physical and emotional pain found refuge in drugs and liquor during the war, and stayed addicted for the rest of their lives. Two generations later, during and after World War I, millions more would find relief from their physical and emotional pain in morphine and heroin. World War II would repeat the pattern. So would Korea and Vietnam. After each war, prohibition was put forward as the solution to the drug and alcohol problems of veterans who had little other recourse to deal with the psychological scars of war. And fear of returning soldiers—usually far overblown—became a handy tool of people who oppose the use of drugs and alcohol.

In the 1870s, Carrie Nation and her ilk smashed up the saloons that gave comfort to Civil War vets. Prohibitionists became mainstream and managed to have booze banned in America by scaring voters and politicians into believing that the trenches of World War I had turned soldiers into vicious men who had to be kept away from liquor for the safety of women and children. Prohibitionists had, during that war, already succeeded in having morphine and opium outlawed. Then, in the 1920s—with liquor Prohibition an obvious failure and a boon to organized crime, prohibitionists set their sites on cannabis.

At that time, few people rose in defense of pot smokers because only a tiny number of Americans had tried the stuff. And those who used it were among the most marginalized people: Mexicans, African-Americans, and poor whites.

Marijuana use in the United States began slowly in the early part of the 20th century. Puerto Rican soldiers, and then Americans who were stationed in the Panama Canal Zone, are reported to have been smoking it by 1916. American soldiers fighting Pancho Villa in 1916 also learned to use it. The drug was relatively new to Mexico, where it first showed up in the 1880s. Possibly its use spread from workers from India brought to the Caribbean, British Honduras, or British Guiana. U.S. soldiers made use of another novelty, the cigarette paper, to roll the first marijuana joints. In the 1920s, marijuana smoking spread from Mexican laborers in the Southwest to blacks in New Orleans. The 1933 *Report of the Military Surgeon* stated, regarding marijuana use among the soldiers in the Canal Zone, that

Marihuana as grown and used on the Isthmus of Panama is a mild stimulant and intoxicant. It is not a "habit forming" drug in the sense that the derivatives of opium, cocaine, and such drugs, are as there are no symptoms of deprivation following its withdrawal. Delinquencies due to marihuana smoking which result in trial by military court are negligible in number when compared with delin-

quencies resulting from the use of alcohol drinks, which is also classed as a stimulant and intoxicant.

The report went on to say that marijuana presented no threat to military discipline, and "that no recommendations to prevent the sale or use of marihuana are deemed advisable."

Despite the military surgeon's findings, the spread of marijuana in New Orleans, up the Mississippi to Chicago, and into the west, troubled U.S. officials. To understand why marijuana was criminalized and the hemp industry died in the crossfire, consider the people who were stigmatized and criminalized; Mexicans, poor blacks, musicians, farm laborers, barge workers, and unemployed city people were virtually the only people smoking pot in America in 1937, when marijuana was banned. In the 1920s, poor people in New Orleans had taken up marijuana smoking, partly as a substitute for alcohol, which was banned, and therefore expensive, under Prohibition. Black deckhands, who did much of the labor on Mississippi barges,

A 19th century print shows middle-class women smoking hashish and opium.

carried it up the river. Very quickly, it jumped from St. Louis to Chicago, then to Great Lakes sailing ships.

My grandfather, who worked on Great Lakes ships in the late 1920s, saw black sailors, who mostly performed the toughest below-deck work, smoking it in the holds of steamships. Like most white sailors of the time, he considered it a low-class alternative to liquor, and believed it beneath him to use—at least publicly. He did try it, but, like many first-time users, didn't find it particularly stimulating.

Within the Prohibition years, marijuana had spread to the Eastern Seaboard. In New York City, a commission appointed by the city's mayor, Fiorello La Guardia, found that about 500 "tea pads" (marijuana speakeasies) were operating in New York City in 1937. All were in Harlem. These were not shabby or dangerous, certainly much more benign than today's crack houses.

LaGuardia's investigators' report described a tea-pad:

The 'tea pad' is furnished according to the clientele it expects to serve. Usually, each 'tea pad' has comfortable furniture, a radio, victrola, or, as in most cases, a rented nickelodeon. The lighting is more or less predominantly dim, with blue predominating. An incense burner is considered part of the furnishings. The walls are frequently decorated with pictures of nude subjects suggestive of perverted sexual practices. The furnishings, as described, are believed to be essential as a setting for those participating in smoking marijuana.

Most 'tea pads' have their trade restricted to the sale of marijuana. Some places did sell marijuana and whisky, and a few places also served as houses of prostitution. Only one 'tea pad' was found which served as a house of prostitution, and in which one could buy marijuana, whisky and opium.

The marijuana smoker derives great satisfaction if he is smoking in the presence of others. His attitude in the 'tea pad' is that of a relaxed individual, free from the anxieties and cares of the realities of life. The 'tea pad' takes on the atmosphere of a congenial social club. The smoker readily engages conversation with strangers, discussing freely his pleasant reactions to the drug and philosophizing on subjects pertaining to life in a manner which, at times, appears to be out of keeping with his intellectual level. A constant observation was the extreme willingness to share and puff on each others' cigarettes. A boisterous, rowdy atmosphere did not prevail and on the rare occasions when there appeared signs indicative of a belligerent smoker, he was ejected or forced to become more tolerant and quiescent. One of the most interesting setups of a 'tea-pad,' which was clearly not along orthodox lines from the business point of view, was a series of pup tents arranged on a rooftop in Harlem. Those present proceeded to smoke their cigarettes in the tents. When the desired effect of the drug had been obtained they all merged into the open and engaged in a discussion of their admiration of the stars and the beauties of nature.

There was bound to be a backlash. Marijuana smokers were the same group of people who scare middle-America now: poor people, blacks, immigrants, and cultural hipsters. Old laws that had made pioneers grow hemp were forgotten, and new laws to outlaw marijuana found their way into the statute books. The chronology suggests the laws came first, then the problems. In 1914, El Paso, Texas, passed the first U.S. ordinance banning the sale or possession of marijuana. Between 1915 and 1937, 40 states passed criminal laws against the selling, possession, and use of the weed. Rocky Mountain and southwestern states, which had large numbers of Mexican transient workers, were the first places to outlaw it, with Texas, New Mexico, Colorado, and Montana the leaders.

One Texas senator didn't mince words about his feelings toward Mexican-Americans, most of whom didn't have the right to vote: "All Mexicans are crazy, and this stuff (marijuana) is what makes them crazy." A proponent of Montana's first marijuana law said, "Give one of these Mexican beet field workers a couple of puffs on a marijuana cigarette and he thinks he is in the bullring at Barcelona."

Connecticut and Rhode Island were the first Eastern states to ban cannabis. New York passed a prohibition act, then repealed it and passed another one. The *New York Times* in an editorial in 1919 said:

No one here in New York uses this drug marijuana. We have only just heard about it from down in the Southwest but we had better prohibit its use before it gets here. Otherwise all the heroin and hard narcotics addicts cut off from their drug by the Harrison Act and all the alcohol drinkers cut off from their drug by 1919 alcohol

Prohibition will substitute this new and unknown drug marijuana for the drugs they used to use.

In the late '30s and early '40s headline writers routinely called marijuana "the killer drug." Henry J. Anslinger, head of the federal Bureau of Narcotics, said, "Marihuana is an addictive drug which produces in its users insanity, criminality, and death." Enterprising lawyers and the gutter press seized on Anslinger's dishonest choice of words. Insanity is more than just a stigmatizing label; it's a legal defense. In the late '30s and early '40s, in five flamboyant murder trials, the defendant's sole defense was that he — or, in the most famous of them, she — was not guilty by reason of insanity for having used marijuana prior to the commission of the crime.

In the most widely followed of the five murders, two women jumped on a Newark, New Jersey, bus and killed and robbed the bus driver. Defense lawyers called a pharmacist who seems to have been a prime candidate for an insanity verdict of his own. He told the jury about his own experiences with pot: "When you used the drug, what happened?" the defense lawyer asked. The drug expert answered: "After two puffs on a marijuana cigarette, I was turned into a bat. My incisor teeth grew six inches long and dripped with blood." He testified that he flew around the room for 15 minutes and then found himself at the bottom of a 200-foot (61-m)-high ink well.

The next day's (April 12, 1936) *Newark Star Ledger* headline read: "Killer Drug Turns Doctor to Bat!"

A trial in New York was, incredibly, more bizarre. A man, who killed two police officers in cold blood after buying but not yet smoking a bag of marijuana, used the marijuana insanity defense. From the time the bag of marijuana came into his room it gave off "homicidal vibrations," so he started killing dogs, cats, and ultimately two police officers. Both defenses succeeded.

These were Prohibition times. But, as the constitutional

amendment that prohibited the manufacture, sale, and consumption of alcohol was repealed and bars reopened, the demonization of "loco weed" continued. State officials from the Southwest, where Mexican laborers smoked the stuff, and from New Orleans, with its community of pot-smoking jazz musicians and poor Cajuns, asked the federal government to enact a national prohibition on marijuana. The press jumped eagerly on the bandwagon.

Anslinger is said to have at first doubted the seriousness of the "problem," but was converted to the anti-pot cause when he realized the boon it would be to his department. In public appearances and radio broadcasts Anslinger asserted that the use of this "evil weed" led to killings, sex crimes, and insanity. He wrote sensational magazine articles with titles like "Marijuana: Assassin of Youth."

For several decades, American publishers churned out dozens of books with titles like *Reefer Girl* and *Marijuana Girl*, in which innocent, young, rich, white women were lured into drug-induced white slavery, prostitution, lives of depravity, or the jazz club. In most of these stories, innocent white girls went into a jazz club and ended up pregnant with a black child (not knowing who the father was because she was either drugged into mental oblivion or was gang-raped), and saddled with a life-long marijuana addiction. The nasty, titillating interracial sexploitation story is a very successful American genre, and the books sold well to white women who could only imagine the wild life of the jazz scene and its intriguing people.

The 1930s was a decade of deep economic suffering, rampant intellectual and political dishonesty, and fear. Middle-class people who still held jobs lived in terror of those who did not and who lived in shanties on the fringes of the cities or wandered the country looking for work. Mussolini and Hitler tapped into this misery as did hundreds of other politicians and bureaucrats who used fear, anger, and scapegoats as weapons against the more helpless parts of society as a way of defusing social unrest. People in countries such as Germany and Italy were much too quick to trade their freedom for false promises of security, and millions would pay the price in the next decade. In America, personal liberty was restricted in return for protection from forces unleashed in the economic collapse.

Marijuana smokers—blacks, Mexicans, people who went to jazz clubs—were easy targets. No lobbyists would argue their case, no politicians would speak out on their behalf. Opium and its derivatives had been banned under the *Harrison Act* of 1914, and, somewhat ironically, Congress was, at that time, worried that people who had supposedly been driven off opiates would turn to cannabis and cocaine. But, by the mid-1930s, opiates were all but forgotten while the anti-marijuana scare campaign was roaring along. A Los Angeles organization called the International Narcotics Education Association put out a brochure in 1936 warning:

Marijuana is a most virile and powerful stimulant. The physiological effect of this drug produces a peculiar psychic exaltation of the nervous system. The stage of exaltation and confusion, more marked in some addicts than in others, is generally followed by a stage of depression...

Prolonged users of marijuana frequently develop a delirious rage which sometimes leads to high crimes, such as assault and murder. Hence marijuana has been called 'the killer drug.' The habitual use of this narcotic poison always causes a very marked mental deterioration and sometimes produces insanity. Hence marijuana is frequently called 'loco weed.' (Loco is the Spanish word for crazy).

While the marijuana habit leads to physical wreckage and mental decay, its effects upon character and morality are even more devastating. The victim frequently undergoes such degeneracy that he will lie and steal without scruple; he becomes utterly untrustworthy and often drifts into the underworld where, with his degenerate companions, he commits high crimes and misdemeanors. Marijuana sometimes gives man the lust to kill unreasonably and without motive. Many cases of assault, rape, robbery and murder are traced to the use of marijuana.

And the campaign spread across the political spectrum. Many left-wing newspapers would later swing around to support decriminalization, but during those New Deal years, they backed all of Franklin Roosevelt's big government plans, including his drug war. The Democrats, at Roosevelt's prodding, pushed anti-marijuana legislation through Congress and shut down the 300-year-old American hemp industry within a few months. Supportive newspapers like the *New York Daily Worker,* helped move things along by printing sensational features about honest citizens whose lives were ruined by the marijuana pushed on them by drug dealers. In January 1937, the paper editorialized:

It destroys the willpower, releases restraints, and promotes insane reactions. Continued use causes the face to become bloated, the eyes bloodshot, the limbs weak and trembling, and the mind sinks into insanity. Robberies, thrill murders, sex crimes and other offenses result... The habit can be cured only by the most severe methods. The addict must be put into an institution, where the drug is gradually withdrawn, his general health is built up, and he is kept there until he has enough willpower to withstand the temptation to again take the weed. The spread of this terrible fad can be stopped only when the unscrupulous criminals trafficking in the drug are rooted out.

The anti-marijuana crusaders won their most important victory in 1937 when the U.S. Supreme Court upheld a Roosevelt administration law requiring owners of some types of machine guns to buy a federal tax stamp. Since the stamp was never offered for sale, the law was, in effect, a ban on a type of gun.

The Supreme Court had allowed the administration to get around the Second Amendment. The new anti-drug bureaucracy decided to invade the states' rights over local criminal law by using the same sleight of hand. A person who wanted a marijuana tax stamp had to pay $1. But he had to have the marijuana in hand to apply for the stamp, although having the marijuana was illegal. And no one was allowed to buy the stamp before producing the marijuana (or any hemp plant or product). The anti-marijuana bill was referred to a House of Representatives committee, where government agents trotted out a circus of dubious witnesses and Anslinger told congressmen, "Marihuana is an addictive drug which produces in its users insanity, criminality, and death."

The hemp industry was killed in the crossfire. Representatives of the rope industry put on a poor defense, saying that the 10,000 acres of U.S. farmland used for hemp were unimportant, that domestic growers could not compete with the plantations of the Far East. The birdseed industry was the biggest lobby fighting the ban, and it didn't stand a chance against Anslinger, an ambitious bureaucrat intent on building a new agency.

The medical profession protested mildly in favor of leaving the drug legal. Its witness told the committee, "The American Medical Association knows of no evidence that marihuana is a dangerous drug." One of the congressmen said, "Doctor, if you can't say something good about what we are trying to do, why don't you go home?" The next congressman to speak added, "Doctor, if you haven't got something better to say than that, we are sick of hearing you."

Democratic congressmen and their party colleagues in the Roosevelt administration remembered that the American Medical Association, from 1932 through 1937, had opposed every piece of New Deal legislation. Republicans, many from states with large populations of Mexican-Americans, supported a federal bill to strengthen the laws already on the books in their home states. And, at the time, hemp and marijuana simply were not important issues with strong constituencies and powerful, well-heeled lobbyists. The bill banning marijuana and hashish was brought onto the floor of the House of Representatives on August 20, 1937. After dealing with one question from a skeptical Republican, the bill was passed without a recorded vote. It sailed through the Senate with no debate at all. No one contested the federal government's incursion into criminal law, a jurisdiction specifically mandated to the states by the Constitution.

For what it's worth, by going through the pretense of holding committee hearings, Congress gave the issue more consideration than some other developed countries. The British parliament had outlawed pot in 1925 after five minutes of debate in the House of Commons between six MPs.

On October 2, 1937, the day the *Marijuana Tax Stamp Act* was enacted, the FBI and Denver, Colorado, police raided the Lexington Hotel and arrested an unlikely-looking drug dealer, Samuel R. Caldwell, a 58-year-old unemployed laborer. Police also picked up a customer, Moses Baca, 26. The next day, both men were indicted by a grand jury, and, on October 5, 1937, Caldwell went into the historical trivia books as the first marijuana seller convicted under U.S. federal law. Baca was found guilty of possession. Anslinger flew in from Washington to watch the trial.

Caldwell's dealings, two marijuana cigarettes, deeply offended Judge Foster Symes, who said as he sentenced the two men:

I consider marijuana the worst of all narcotics, far worse than the use of morphine or cocaine. Under its influence men become beasts. Marijuana destroys life itself. I have no sympathy with those who sell this weed. The government is going to enforce this new law to the letter.

Caldwell was sentenced to four years of hard labor in Leavenworth Penitentiary, and a $1000 fine. Baca received 18 months' incarceration.

Anslinger, then head of an organization that prided itself on issuing its agents a badge, a tommy gun, and hand grenades, became as paranoid as the most doped-out addict. In his mind, America's "drug problem" was sponsored by evil foreign powers. During World War II, the Japanese were said to be pushing pot to sap American youth of its will to fight. Then, during the Cold War, it was the Communists who were undermining America's youth by turning them on to drugs. Congressmen kept buying Anslinger's fantasies, passing the *Boggs Act* in 1953, at the height of the McCarthy witchhunt, which made marijuana possession as serious a crime as possession of heroin. Three years later, Anslinger came up with the argument that marijuana is a stepping-stone to heroin and was rewarded with the *Narcotic Control Act*, which increased sentences even more.

In 1938, after the passage of the *Marijuana Tax Stamp Act*, Canada's politicians identified the marijuana menace and protected Canadians from it. In fact, it was quite a stretch for them to find any domestic marijuana problem at all. The first time the RCMP mentioned marijuana, it was to reassure Canadians: just days after Congress passed the *Marijuana Tax Stamp Act*, the Mounties told newspaper reporters that Canada was pretty much free of the drug said to

Samuel R. Caldwell, the first American convicted of selling marijuana, spent four years in Leavenworth.

be the cause of thousands of crimes in the United States, particularly murder. On June 12, 1937, the *Globe and Mail* ran this:

Marijuana, peddled to many young people in the United States, causes insanity in many cases. Its effect is often unpredictable. It has been known to turn quiet, respectable youths into raving murderers, seeking victims to satisfy their delusions.

It took another two months for Canada's Parliament to come to grips with the non-menace facing the nation. As the Nazis made their final lunge for Austria and Britain's Lord Halifax made the empty threat that his country was ready to take on Hitler, debate began in Canada's House of Commons on an anti-marijuana, anti-hemp law. "Marijuana is by no means a new drug," Pensions and National Health Minister C. G. Powers, a newly minted expert on the problem, told his colleagues. "It has been known since the time of Homer. It was formerly known as hashish, and is exceedingly stimulating." The minister went on to talk about how the weed had made it into Canada. It had slipped into the country during World War I, when it was used for making twine. Liberal members of Parliament criticized their own government for its "sham" drug protection policies. J. K. Blair, a Liberal, worried that evildoers were spiking ordinary cigarettes with marijuana. "I think a great number of our highway accidents are caused by smoking cigarettes with dope in them," he said. No one challenged that claim, but the House of Commons did stop short of adopting an amendment to ban codeine.

Later, as the Canadian Senate discussed the bill, the government realized it would have no source of hemp rope for the war that was obviously coming. Ottawa finally realized Canada still needed hemp, and that supplies from the U.S. had been cut off. The government came up with a licensing system that served well during wartime and was revived in 1994, when the government allowed hemp growing to start up again.

In Summer 1938, as Japanese troops encircled 100,000 Chinese soldiers northwest of Shanghai and Stalin's prosecutors presented their case against 21 Russians held on trumped-up charges of murdering novelist Maxim Gorky, police in

Hamilton, Ontario, sat down to smoke some pot. They lit up some marijuana "just to attune their nasal powers so in future by merely sniffing, they'll be able to detect the drug," the city's police chief, E. K. Goodman, said. Cops had never found the weed in the city, but the chief wanted his men to be able to catch pot smokers. The Hamilton cops had to mooch some marijuana from the Royal Canadian Mounted Police. The city police put some marijuana in a tin can, set it on fire, and took turns inhaling the potentially murder-inspiring smoke. "Even in a crowded room where cigars, good and bad, pipes and cigarettes are sending up a smoke screen the trained nostrils of the officers, with the certainty of efficient bloodhounds, will be able to single out the marijuana addict and enable them to get their man," the *Toronto Globe and Mail* crowed in a front-page story on March 11, 1938.

Two months after the House of Commons began its debate on marijuana, Toronto cops picked up their first pot dealers. Duncan Campbell, John Short, and Robert Tubman were caught selling several marijuana cigarettes to a woman for 50 cents apiece.

Finally, a Canadian murderer came forward to admit that marijuana had inspired him to commit his crime. Thomas Bryans, facing the gallows for shooting a hood named Norman Ford in the Toronto suburb of York Township, used the "reefer madness" defense in his trial. But it turned out Bryans came up with the excuse by overhearing cop talk at the police station.

"Bryans, condemned murderer, is said to blame his downfall on smoking marijuana cigarettes. But murder is a very old crime, and marijuana is one of the most modern of drugs," a Toronto paper quipped.

Conspiracy theorists see the banning of marijuana and hemp as part of a plot between the inflammatory Hearst newspapers, the synthetic fiber industry, and the U.S. government. In his 1998 book, *The Emperor Wears No Clothes*, author Jack Herer accuses William Randolph Hearst, the DuPont Company, and Harry J. Anslinger of conspiring to make cannabis illegal. Hearst, he says, gained by selling newspapers detailing marijuana horrors, and from sales from the press baron's string of newsprint mills; DuPont and other chemical companies would have new markets for their synthetics; and Anslinger would get his bureaucratic fiefdom.

But Herer's argument is not completely convincing. There may have been motives for Hearst and the chemical companies to want marijuana banned and hemp off the market, and Anslinger certainly had plans for a sweeping federal drug agency, but motives in themselves do not prove conspiracy. The hemp ban came at a time when steamships had replaced sailing ships. Synthetic fabrics could compete with high-priced imports like silk, and, in a couple of years, nylon and other soft fibers would take over the stocking market and offer consumers a cheap substitute for cotton. By the time hemp was banned, very little of it was being grown in the United States, and most of that was used for birdseed.

In the Depression summers of 1937 and 1938, police across America began rooting out wild hemp, roadside marijuana patches, and tea pads. Around Detroit, police found patches of the stuff growing wild around the city, and burned five tons in one day. Michigan Attorney General Raymond Starr was relieved that so much pot had been found. "Smokers of these drugged cigarettes are turned into raving maniacs. They are led to commit the most brutal crimes. The danger is particularly great since peddlers concentrate on school children," he said.

That claim was refuted—along with most of Anslinger's "evidence,"—by an expert panel assembled by New York mayor Fiorello La Guardia in 1939. During its four-year study, the New York committee interviewed high school principals. Most had never seen signs of marijuana use. In the few schools where pot had been found, teachers said it was, at most, a minor problem. To see if the educators had a grip on the "problem," the committee sent spies into schoolyards. Agents lurked on nearby streets (where some were picked up by police acting on complaints that suspicious strangers were ogling students). Marijuana use, they found, was minimal. The only people selling cigarettes to kids were adults making money by peddling individual tobacco cigarettes to students who didn't have enough money for a whole pack.

Meanwhile, the hemp industry in Kentucky and Minnesota died. Shiploads of fiber arrived from the Far East. Four years after Congress effectively killed the American hemp business, the Japanese captured the Philippines and Java, the last of the world's major hemp plantation regions. In 1942 the United States government decided it would be necessary to produce large quantities of hemp fiber domestically to meet the armed forces' demands for rope, binder twine, and other types of cordage. The program was assigned to the Department of Agriculture. It arranged to have the Commodity Credit Corporation, a New Deal agency set up in the Depression, build 42 hemp mills in the Midwest. Farmers were dubious about taking up hemp farming. They worried that they would lose money if their fields weren't sown in corn. Most of the farmers had never grown hemp and weren't sure how to do it. The government had to use a mix of persuasion and grants to get farmers to join the program.

The first crops were sown in the spring of 1943. Most of the hemp fields were small, about 10 acres, but they were money-makers for the farmers. Most replanted hemp in 1944 and 1945. Then, with the drop in demand for ship rope and the reopening of the Far East hemp supply, the domestic hemp farms switched back to grain crops, the wartime hemp mills shut down, and the experiment died.

While Anslinger did not share J. Edgar Hoover's penchant for cross-dressing, Anslinger did emulate the FBI director's fetish for keeping files on well-known entertainers whose behavior seemed un-American. Anslinger disliked jazz and kept a special file, "Marijuana and Musicians," filled with reports on band members who played with Cab Calloway, Louis Armstrong, Les Brown, Count Basie, Jimmy Dorsey, and Duke Ellington, among others. He wanted to bust all of the top jazz musicians, but his agents weren't able to infiltrate their tight society.

Anslinger retired in 1962, just before Middle America discovered marijuana. He had been able to convince many states to pass "little *Boggs* acts" with penalties for marijuana possession or sale tougher than those demanded by federal law. A person caught with pot in Louisiana could end up in prison for five to 99 years. Missouri, a place with far fewer smokers, allowed judges to send people convicted of a second offense to jail for life. Pot dealers could get the electric chair in Georgia on a second conviction for selling marijuana to minors, but there's no record that it actually happened. Instead, most of these laws were just drying on the books when middle-class kids started getting picked up for possession. It was fine for Mexicans, blacks, and jazz lovers to end up spending 99 years on a Louisiana chain gang for possession, but the kids of doctors and lawyers surely deserved better.

As a result, presidents John F. Kennedy, Lyndon Johnson, and Richard Nixon all appointed committees to look into the drug issues. All of them came back with the same findings of the La Guardia Committee: marijuana doesn't lead to violent crime or heroin use. Enforcement of simple possession laws slacked off in many cities, especially in California and the Northeast. President Jimmy Carter wanted to decriminalize marijuana, but his successor declared the "War on Drugs."

The *Comprehensive Crime Control Act* of 1984, the *Anti-Drug Abuse Act* of 1986, and the *Anti-Drug Abuse Amendment Act* of 1988 raised federal penalties for marijuana possession, cultivation, and trafficking. Sentences were determined by the quantity of the drug involved. The law punished "conspiracies" and "attempts" with the same sentences as completed acts. Possession of 100 marijuana plants carried the same sentence as possession of 3 ounces (100 grams) of heroin.

Marijuana is now a Schedule I controlled substance in the U.S. Officially, it has a high potential for abuse, no officially accepted medicinal uses, and no safe level of use even under medical supervision. Heroin, LSD, and peyote are other Schedule I drugs. Cocaine and phencyclidine (PCP) are not as bad. They're listed in Schedule II, so doctors may prescribe them (although you're unlikely to find one who will). Reagan's laws prohibit anyone to use the U.S. Postal Service or other interstate shippers for the advertisement, import, or export of marijuana paraphernalia. Shipping roach clips, water pipes, and some cigarette papers across state lines can result in jail time and a $100,000 fine. The government can, and does, seize real estate, money, cars, and any other property it deems is used in the marijuana trade or bought with profits from it. The government sometimes takes this property even after a person has been acquitted. It goes after its loot in civil court, where it must only prove a balance of probabilities, rather than guilty beyond a reasonable doubt.

(In Canada, the government works from a double standard. It seizes "grow houses" used for hydroponic pot growing but leaves back-to-the-land hippies and other rural pot growers with their farms.)

A convicted marijuana offender may face the revocation or denial of more than 460 federal benefits, including student loans, small-business loans, professional licenses, and farm subsidies. In international smuggling cases, the offender's passport can be revoked.

Yet, while the federal government jacks up its penalties and seizes the property of pot growers and dealers, the states send mixed messages. Some have loosened their possession laws, while others are more draconian than federal statues. New York State's laws make the possession of slightly less than an ounce (30 grams) of marijuana punishable by a $100 fine. In Nevada, possessing any amount of marijuana is a felony. In Montana, selling a pound of marijuana as a first offense could lead to a life sentence. In New Mexico, selling 10,000 pounds of marijuana as a first offense could be punished with a prison term of no more than three years.

In Kentucky, the last great hemp-growing state, possessing products made of hemp fibers, such as paper and clothing, carries the same penalties associated with an equivalent weight of marijuana. These laws have been challenged by actor Woody Harrelson and other hemp activists. While a jury let Harrelson go in August 2000 on charges of possession of marijuana for planting four hemp seeds, the state's Supreme Court upheld the law itself (see Decriminalization and Reaction).

Laws vary from county to county in Kentucky. Some impose fines for possession of small amounts of marijuana. Some impose jail sentences, send convicts to boot camps, and seize cars. Hyped by shows such as *Cops*, paramilitary-style SWAT teams have kept themselves busy raiding the homes of suspected drug dealers. Here are just a few of the recent attacks on Americans:

- September 13, 2000: In Modesto, California, a SWAT team burst into the home of 11-year-old Alberto Sepulveda to serve a drug trafficking warrant on his father, a suspected marijuana dealer. While rounding up his family, officers ordered Alberto to lie on the floor, face down, which the boy did. Seconds later, an officer accidentally fired a shotgun that was trained on Alberto's back, killing him.
- September 29, 1999: Denver SWAT officers killed 45-year-old Mexican immigrant Ismael Mena in what turned out to be a drug raid on the wrong house. The city paid the Mena family $400,000 to avoid a wrongful-death lawsuit.

- February 13, 1999: At 1:25 a.m. in Osawatomie, Kansas, police set off a flash-bang grenade before bursting into the home of Willie Heard, looking for cocaine. The explosion startled Heard's 16-year-old daughter, who screamed. Heard, in his bedroom and thinking his daughter was in danger, grabbed a .22 bolt-action rifle. When police smashed into the bedroom they saw Heard with the rifle and shot him dead. The entire incident lasted 11 seconds.
- July 12, 1998: Acting on a single tip that Pedro Oregon Navarro was dealing marijuana, a team of Houston officers charged into the apartment of the 22-year-old, who picked up a handgun. The officers unleashed 30 shots, hitting Navarro 12 times, nine times in the back. No drugs were found.
- March 13, 1996: In Oxnard, California, the deployment of a flash-bang grenade during a drug raid created such confusion that SWAT team commander Daniel Christian killed Officer James Jensen Jr. with three shotgun blasts to his side. The city later settled a lawsuit filed by Jensen's family for $3.5 million.
- April 15, 1995: A Dodge County, Wisconsin, SWAT team raided the trailer of Scott Bryant, a 29-year-old technical college student who was living in Beaver Dam with his 8-year-old son. As the first officer to smash through the door was placing Bryant on a couch to be handcuffed, Detective Robert Neuman rushed in and delivered a fatal bullet to Bryant's chest. A small amount of marijuana was found in the trailer. While no charges were ever filed against the detective, the county paid $950,000 to settle a federal civil rights lawsuit filed by Bryant's family.
- August 9, 1994: In Riverside County, California, 87-year-old Donald Harrison and his 77-year-old wife, Elsie, were asleep in their mobile home when deputies smashed in looking for drugs. Donald died of a heart attack four days later.

It turned out that police had the wrong place, despite a detailed description of the suspect's home, which was a different color from the Harrisons' trailer.

Federal agents and local narcotics police bring government into disrepute by conducting violent raids on small-time dealers, seizing, at the Canadian and Mexican borders, people's cars because a marijuana seed is found by a sniffer dog, and, in New Jersey, bribing hotel workers to monitor guests. For over seven years, New Jersey state police recruited hotel managers to allow them access to registration forms and credit card receipts without a warrant. Narcotics officers paid cash to hotel employees who tipped police about people who paid for their rooms in cash, received too many phone calls, or spoke Spanish. The cops offered $1000 for any tip that led to an arrest, and promised the hotels that their complicity would not be revealed. State troopers ran seminars for hotel staff, training them to scrutinize guests for suspicious behavior. Although the police vehemently deny targeting Hispanics, they got around the race issue by asking staff to pay special attention to guests "who speak Spanish."

The nasty racial overtones of the original marijuana ban continue. The War on Drugs is also a war against the inner-city poor. The arrest rate—the rate per thousand of people who, after being found in possession of small amounts of marijuana, are issued a citation—shows that minorities are much more likely to feel the full sting of the law. Among the 63 metro core counties, only three report white arrest rates greater than black arrest rates for marijuana possession: Detroit, Honolulu, and Bakersfield, California.

In 1986, after Nancy Reagan took up the drug war as her own pet project, the president ordered drug tests for all federal employees. Thousands of people had their careers ruined by error-plagued drug testing. For example, one commonly used test showed a false positive for marijuana if there were traces of the painkillers Nuprin or Advil in the sample. The common cold medication Contac spurred a false positive for amphetamines. The quinine in tonic water was mistaken as a marker for heroin. Personal liberty was sacrificed for the empty promise that the troubles in America's cities could be cleaned up by making national park rangers and tax auditors hand over a urine sample. Drug testing may make sense for air traffic controllers, but many low-level clerks, postal workers, and laborers were caught in the net.

The drug war continues. In 2002, the government spent more on it than on the fight against terrorism. Police in America arrested an estimated 734,498 persons for marijuana violations in 2000, according to the Federal Bureau of Investigation's annual *Uniform Crime Report.* That total was the highest ever recorded by the FBI, and comprises just under half of the drug arrests in the United States. Of those charged with marijuana violations, almost 88 percent—some 646,042 Americans—were charged with possession. The other 88,456 people were charged with "sale/manufacture," a category that includes all cultivation offenses—even those where the marijuana was being grown for personal or medical use. The number of marijuana arrests far exceeded the total number of arrests for all violent crimes combined, including murder, manslaughter, rape, robbery, and aggravated assault. Between 1990 and 2000, nearly 5.9 million Americans have been arrested on marijuana charges, a number greater than the entire populations of Alaska, Delaware, the District of Columbia, Montana, North Dakota, South Dakota, Vermont, and Wyoming combined. In 2000, American taxpayers paid $10 billion for police, prosecutors, public defenders, jails, and other costs of the drug war.

Samuel Caldwell was a pioneer for the many who followed him to jail: sports heroes Kareem Abdul-Jabbar, Robert Parish, Fergy Jenkins, Orlando Cepeda, Vernon Maxwell, Isaiah Rider, Allen Iverson, Mookie Blaylock, and Marcus Camby have been caught in the net.

So was actor Robert Mitchum, whose career was nearly destroyed when he was arrested by Anslinger's men in a 1948 stakeout in Laurel Canyon, California. Bob Denver, who had enough problems living down his role as the title character on the popular '60s television show *Gilligan's Island*, was arrested in 1998 after a package containing two ounces of marijuana was delivered to his West Virginia house. Filmmaker Oliver Stone, who made *JFK*, *Platoon*, and *Born on the Fourth of July*, was pulled over by police officers for driving erratically and subsequently arrested when hashish and painkillers were found in his car.

Matthew McConaughey, who starred in *Dazed and Confused* and *Amistad*, was arrested in his Texas home after neighbors complained about noise.

Anslinger deliberately targeted drummer Gene Kruppa in a 1943 sting against jazz musicians. The arrest dogged the musician for the rest of his career. By the time singer Whitney Houston was caught with half an ounce (15 grams) of marijuana when she boarded an airplane in Hawaii, celebrity pot possession was old news. Beatles John Lennon, Paul McCartney, and George Harrison; rappers Snoop Doggy Dogg and Chuck D; soul-music icon James Brown; country crooner Willie Nelson; rocker David Lee Roth; guitarists Carlos Santana and Freddie Fender; rockers David Bowie and Iggy Pop have all been arrested, and, presumably, rehabilitated.

Amazingly, only two members of the Grateful Dead (neither of them Jerry Garcia) were busted, and a big raid on their party house was botched. Many of the celebrities present managed to beat their charges or were given light sentences, but the publicity surrounding their arrests probably hurt their careers. One rock great, Elvis Presley, evaded the dragnet and was made an honorary special agent of the Drug Enforcement Administration by President Richard Nixon. Six years later he was found dead on his toilet. He had enough prescription drugs in his system to open a small pharmacy.

In the past 25 years, farmers, industry owners, consumers, and politicians have taken another look at hemp and found that the haste of the Depression-era legislators was an expensive mistake: a crop plant that offers both fiber and high-quality oil should not have been cast aside so quickly. By the 1980s, hemp advocates and agricultural scientists in Europe and Canada were developing dozens of uses for the plant. They've been so successful that the arguments against the reintroduction of hemp into the fields of the United States seem to be based more on prejudice and stubborn anti-cannabis zeal than on rational concepts of public protection. The Declaration of Independence and the Constitution, printed and distributed 200 years ago on hemp paper, are mocked by the actions of the people who use America's drug war to maintain a ban on a plant that was grown on the farms of Washington and Jefferson.

HEMP MAKES A COMEBACK

Every summer across North America, towns and villages organize events to draw tourists and break up the long weeks of boredom endured by school-aged kids. Some communities hold fairs and flower shows. Those in wine regions celebrate the grape. In apple country, there's usually at least one late-summer event. One community in the U.S. Midwest salutes the hobo. Several others on the continent celebrate Elvis Presley.

In Barrie, Ontario, which is in the center of Canada's (and, so far, North America's) hemp-growing region, it's cannabis. Barrie is a town of 125,000 people an hour's drive north of Toronto, and is known as the gateway to Ontario's Cottage Country. Just north of Barrie, in the crossroads hamlet of Dalston, is Hempola, the continent's pioneering hemp-growing company. And, when it opens its gates to the public in the second week of August, people get a chance to see what hemp can do.

Visitors to the Hempola Family Farm Festival walk along educational "trivia" trails in the hemp fields, take hayrides, sample nutritious and delicious hemp foods, listen in at seminars, talk with experts and hemp product manufacturers, listen to live music, and play in a children's section. If it rains, events are held in giant canvas tents and the world's first hemp straw "roundhouse."

Hempola is doing well. Its owners have made an ordinary farm with a lovely old house and an 1858 heritage barn into the Mecca of the hemp movement. During the festival, people get a chance to see the spin-off industries that are cashing in on the revival of hemp: Fast Fuel, *Health'N Vitality* magazine, Hemptown Clothing, Friendly Stranger, *Canadian Natural Retailer* magazine, *The Healthy Shopper* magazine, and Embassy Food Specialties.

Hempola and the other Canadian companies that have embraced the hemp plant have had only nine harvests since permission to grow industrial hemp was granted in Canada in 1994. They've had their share of frustrations, but the crop's starting to pay off. Hempola Valley Farms, which grows hemp and buys hemp oil seeds from other growers for its own products, has been able to help other farmers find markets for fiber. As well, it's become so efficient that, in 2002, it was able to cut the retail price of cold-pressed hempseed oil by 20 percent.

This small Japanese hashish pipe was made in the 18th century for a wealthy woman.

Kelly Smith, co-founder of Hempola, says "all indications tell us that in the next few years we should be experiencing close to twice the yield of hempseed as we and our farmers learn how to best manage this new crop. We have to recognize that four years of crop experience with hemp is very little. Other crops like corn and canola have had anywhere from 40 to over 100 years of cultivation." Before 1998, Hempola imported seed from China.

"Our landed cost was over one dollar per pound. The market price for domestic Canadian-grown hempseed today is about one-third the cost...and Canadian farmers are making a good profit compared to most commodity crops like wheat and soybeans. In 1996 a bottle of Hempola was around $25. Today, the same size bottle of Hempola is anywhere from $9 to $12, depending on where you shop."

The hemp movement has been gaining ground in fits and starts. Since Canada legalized production of industrial hemp, entrepreneurial Americans have created a $100 million per year industry manufacturing hemp products. Americans can now buy hemp paper, clothes, bags, shoes, and even hemp "tofu."

In 1998 the American Farm Bureau Federation called hemp "one of the most promising crops in half a century." Fashion giants Adidas, Ralph Lauren, and Calvin Klein recently added hempen goods to their clothing lines; Klein also predicted that hemp would become "the fiber of choice" for the home furnishing industry. The number of stores selling hemp products has exploded in recent years and the number of American manufacturers producing a variety of hemp-based goods ranging from socks to skin care is now estimated at over 1,000.

A current dilemma for North American hemp growing is that we have lost the genetic diversity of hemp strains, the machinery, and the know-how of raising the crop. But, at the same time, hemp agriculture is unencumbered by antiquation. In places where it's been legalized, hemp agriculture is thriving, farmers and processors have overcome start-up problems, and there has been none of the problems, such as theft of plant flowers, predicted by opponents of hemp.

Farmers have found that hemp is now a profitable and easy-to-process crop. It's also beneficial to the land as a nitrogen fixer. In his 1975 textbook, *Modern Weed Control*, A. S. Crafts wrote about hemp's potential as a weed-smothering crop. And, in 1890, Charles Dodge, the federal Director of Fiber, wrote *it is certain that hemp contributes more than any other crop towards repairing the damage done by its own growth through the return of the leaves to the soil, besides other matters while it is undergoing the process of retting. Hemp is an admirable weed killer and in flax countries is sometimes employed as a crop in rotation, to precede flax because it puts the soil in so good condition.*

There will be little trouble with weeds if the first crop is well destroyed by the spring plowing, for hemp generally occupies all the ground giving weeds but little chance to intrude... In proof of this, a North River farmer a few years ago made the statement that thistles heretofore had mastered him in a certain field, but after sowing it with hemp not a thistle survived, and while ridding his land of this pest the hemp yielded him nearly $60 per acre where previously nothing valuable could be produced.

The economic benefits of hemp agriculture have become obvious to many politicians, especially those with large farming constituencies. Farmers across the continent have been mauled by low commodity prices, which, in real terms, are the lowest they've been in modern history. At the same time, they've had to pay much more for fertilizers, pesticides, and seeds. Farmers also have to compete with colleagues who have succumbed to the pressure to use genetically modified seeds to try to raise yields and break even.

Many American farmers are ready to grow hemp, once the government relents. They've joined organizations like Hemp Industries Association (HIA), a farmers and hemp-manufacturers group started in 1992, which lobbies for fair and equal treatment of industrial hemp and pushes for a level playing field to compete with other natural resources and synthetics. The HIA wants changes in government policies to encourage global production of hemp as a raw material for industry.

Legalization of hemp won't solve the American farm crisis, but it could help thousands of farmers stay on the land. Canada, realizing the potential to take marginal land out of traditional crops, allows hemp growing under tight controls and even encouraged tobacco farmers in southern Ontario to switch to hemp. Hawaii has not only passed legislation allowing for hemp-growing trials but also planted the first legal hemp crop since the 1950s. However, traditional hemp-growing areas in the U.S., especially Kentucky, are still under a hemp-growing ban, despite support for the crop among local farmers and hemp activists.

Nevertheless, growing hemp is currently legal in more than 25 countries including Canada, Germany, England, France, Holland, Spain, the Russian Federation, Hungary, Romania, China, and Thailand.

And what's being done with the crops, especially in North America and Western Europe, is nothing short of incredible.

CHAPTER 2

Uses for Cannabis

FOOD

It's a hot day at the Bancroft Gemboree, a mineral and crystal show held in cottage country north of Toronto on the first weekend of August. Dozens of rock and jewelry dealers have their collections set up on tables outside the local hockey arena. So does HempDreams, a hemp ice cream company based in Killaloe, a small Ontario town with a large counterculture population. Killaloe is about 45 miles (75 kilometers) away, near the east end of Algonquin Park. Hippies started moving to the area in the mid-1960s, drawn by cheap land and privacy. Now, among the craftspeople, musicians, writers, and pot growers of the community, there's strong support for the legalization of hemp and a burgeoning local industry that uses hemp to make food and crafts.

Hemp ice cream is just one of the products that can be made from oil pressed from the seeds of the plant. Even with all of the safeguards mandated by Canadian law—licensing, fencing, security—and the scarcity of hemp seed, HempDreams is able to sell its product in that Bancroft parking lot for about the same price as regular ice cream. Not only does hemp ice cream appeal to those people who prefer hemp on principle, but there's a huge market among people who are lactose intolerant and can't digest the milk sugars in regular ice cream. And hemp ice cream, along with all of the other foods that can be made from the plant, addresses a need among vegans and vegetarians.

Is hemp ice cream tasty? Our family of four put it to the test. HempDreams makes three flavors: vanilla, natural maple, and chocolate. With our three-year-old, the chocolate was quite popular, both as food and as a full facial cosmetic. It was also the favorite of our seven-year-old. I liked both the chocolate and the vanilla. My wife, a nutritionist, said she found the flavors a bit weak, but quickly added that it was far better tasting than any other non-dairy ice cream she'd tried.

To make ice cream from hemp you use the oil from the seeds. Hemp seeds grow in flowering buds located at the top of the plant and at the end of the larger branches. Depending on the strain, each plant can produce from 500 to 25,000 seeds. Even after Prohibition, sterilized hemp seed is still used occasionally in bird food. The oil makes bird feathers shine, and the seeds are high in nutrients. In fact, the testimony of parakeet fanciers that their birds would not sing unless they were fed hemp seeds convinced Congress to make an exception for them in 1937. Hemp seeds, which can't be made into food for the American people, are fine for the country's birds as long as the seeds are sterilized. The seed husks contain trace levels of THC, not enough to stimulate humans or birds.

There are about 50 essential nutrients for human health, including two essential fatty acids (fats), eight essential amino acids (proteins), 13 vitamins, 20 or 21 minerals, a source of energy (calories), and water. Foods usually contain some, but not all, of the nutrients we need. Even among people in developed countries, deficiencies in essential nutrients are quite common; more than 60 percent of North Americans get less than the recommended daily amount of one or more essential nutrients. People in affluent nations eat too many processed foods: refined white flour, white rice, white sugar, and refined fats. The refining processes strip away most of the vitamins, minerals, and essential fatty acids, leaving the calories without the nutrients.

Human nutrition is a science that's awash in controversies, theories, and ideologies. Hemp activists would like to see their favorite plant assume the title of "nature's perfect food." At the very least, hemp seeds hold some of the nutrients that are too often left out of North American and European diets. Hemp seeds contain 25 percent high-quality protein and 40 percent fat. Hemp oil has a remarkable fatty acid profile, being high in desirable omega-3 and omega-6 fatty acids and also delivering some GLA (gamma-linolenic acid) that is absent from the fats we normally eat. All of these compounds are beneficial to health. Deficiency in omega-3 fatty acids can lead to skin diseases, heart disease, and inflammatory conditions along with premature aging and disorders of the central nervous system. Omega-3 fatty acids also promote cardiovascular health and are believed to help protect against many cancers, including breast cancer.

Hemp oil contains 57 percent linoleic (LA) and 19 percent linolenic (LNA) acids, in the 3:1 ratio that matches our nutritional needs. These are the essential fatty acids (EFAs) that our bodies cannot make. The best sources are oils from freshly ground grains and whole seeds, but EFAs are fragile and quickly lost in processing. EFAs are the building blocks of longer-chain fats, such as eicosapentaenoic (EPA) and acid (DHA) that occur naturally in the fat of cold-water fish like sardines, mackerel, salmon, bluefish, herring, and, to a lesser extent, tuna.

President Dwight Eisenhower invited Civil War buffs to a re-enactment of the Battle of the Hemp Bales.

In our bodies, essential amino acids and EFAs work together to produce energy. They combine to form lipoproteins, which make up the membranes of every cell in our bodies. Lipoproteins also form the hemoglobin in our blood and move fats through our bodies. To maintain healthy bodies, it's important to balance our intake of protein and essential fatty acids. The average North American consumes more than enough protein and not enough EFAs to balance it out. Increasing EFAs in the diet can decrease the toxicity of extra protein, and also reverse many of the common health problems we have today, including heart disease and cancer.

Adding these nutrients to the diet seems to lower risks of heart attacks because omega-3 fatty acids, one of the EFAs, reduce the clotting tendency of the blood and improve cholesterol profiles. They also have a natural anti-inflammatory effect that makes them useful for people with arthritis and autoimmune disorders. In western diets, Omega-3s come primarily from salmon, herring, sardines, and other oily fish.

Oil from cold-pressed hemp seeds is a prime vegetable source for complete proteins. The oil contains all eight essential amino acids, is more easily digested, and tastes better than its vegetable-protein rival, soy. Hemp seeds are the only edible seeds to contain a very rare nutrient—gamma linoleic acid, or GLA, which is an active agent in lowering cholesterol.

Whole hemp seeds can be used for snacks, in cooking, even roasted and mixed in coffee. Processed hemp seeds can be used to make non-dairy milk, various styles of cheese and ice cream, or ground up and used in spreads similar to peanut butter. After the seeds have been crushed for their oil, they can be processed into protein powder, flour, and veggie burgers, or even used to brew beer.

Unrefined hemp oil can be taken daily as a dietary supplement or used in salad dressings and cooking in place of other vegetable oils. For maximum nutrition value, hemp oil should be stored in the refrigerator and used quickly.

Many people eat the seeds plain or add them to other foods, including baked goods, baked potatoes, or dried fruit and nut mixtures.

Because it's usually grown without pesticides, hemp protein is equal or superior to soy protein. Whole hemp seeds contain about 23 percent protein; hulled seeds contain around 30 to 31 percent. Hemp seeds are hulled to remove the outer fibrous shell, to make products such as hemp milk, cheese, and tofu.

The protein in hemp seeds also contains the highest amount (65 percent) of edestin protein among plant seeds. Edestin is a type of globular protein, classified by their globe-like shapes, that is easily digested and utilized by the body. All enzymes and antibodies in the body are globular proteins, as are many of the proteins found in blood and hormones that carry out many of the important life functions in our bodies. Animal-feeding studies have found that edestin proteins are capable of serving as the sole source of protein in animal diets. Because of their high quality protein, hemp seeds were used like soybeans for premium cattle feed in the United States until they became unavailable in the 1950s. As more people get more of their protein from plants, it makes sense to look at the plant foods that provide the best nutrition for other herbivores.

Many of the diseases that afflict developed nations, including heart disease and cancer, have dramatically increased in the past century. Researchers now recognize that the increases in these diseases probably correspond to overall changes in our diets, especially to the consumption of processed fats and excess animal products. Many of our current health problems are thought to be related to fatty degeneration diseases, which come from eating too much bad fat and not enough good fat.

For example, the proportion of saturated fat (usually from animal products) we consume is often too high. Second, we eat too many refined and processed fats. These fats usually start off with good sources of plant oils, high in polyunsaturates; however, the processes used to make them more shelf-stable can convert them from nutrients into toxins.

Essential fatty acids are inherently unstable, and easily react to heat, light, and oxygen. These reactions can convert them from healthy molecules into unhealthy ones. In order to obtain oil that is nutritious, plant seeds should be processed with great care in the absence of heat, light, and oxygen, then stored in opaque bottles at reduced temperatures. Unfortunately, the processing of most commercially available oils is the exact opposite.

Manufacturers are concerned with making fats and oils more

stable, so they have a long shelf life and can be stored for up to a year without turning rancid. They often subject natural oils to severe processing with high heat and chemicals, with no care to exclude light or oxygen. These processes remove the unstable molecules, which, unfortunately, also contain the nutrients.

The worst case is partially hydrogenated oils, where almost all of the nutrients are removed by the formation of large amounts of unnatural molecules that can be extremely toxic to our bodies, including high amounts of trans-fatty acids. Trans-fatty acids were once polyunsaturated fats which have been processed into saturated fats. Most margarines and shortenings are partially hydrogenated oils, and most contain high amounts of trans-fatty acids.

In 2003, the hemp food business got a boost when officials of the 30th annual American Music Awards handed out gift bags containing hemp-based foods and cosmetics to all the nominees, presenters, and performers.

These gift bags, each worth $30,000, were put together by Dick Clark Productions, which does the same thing for the Golden Globe ceremonies. Because of the U.S. government ban on most hemp products, Dick Clark's people had to go to Canada to get hemp goodies. Along with things like scooters and tickets to rafting trips in Chile, each bag held Hempola Honey Dijon Dressing, Lip Balm, and High Protein Pancake Mix.

FIBER

The ropes that held together the parachute that saved George Bush Sr.'s life in World War II were made of hemp fiber. That parachute was made in the very last days of America's hemp industry, but so much more could have been done with the slandered plant if the nation's creativity had been let loose. Just before Congress killed off the wartime industry, there had been signs of breakthroughs. For instance, Henry Ford dreamed that someday automobiles would be grown from the soil. In 1941 the Ford Motor Company produced an experimental automobile with a plastic body composed of 70 percent cellulose fibers from hemp. The car body could absorb blows 10 times better than steel without denting and was designed to run on hemp fuel. However, Detroit isn't enthusiastic about cars that don't rust and don't use gasoline.

Industrial hemp could reduce cloth manufacturer's dependence on cotton, which is typically grown with large amounts of harmful chemicals; about 50 percent of the pesticides used in the world are sprayed on cotton. Hemp grows well in a wide variety of climates and soils and requires far less fertilizer and pesticides than most commercial crops. European farms have found that, as part of a careful program of crop rotation, it's very beneficial to soils. If, like many North American crops, it's grown in a monoculture operation—the replanting of a crop in the same fields year after year, with few fallow seasons—then like any crop, it does need pesticides and fertilizers.

One acre (0.4 hectares) of hemp can produce as much usable fiber as four acres (1.6 hectares) of trees or two acres (0.8 hectares) of cotton. Hemp fabric requires fewer chemicals than cotton to process and is stronger and longer lasting. Hemp should be worth $500 per acre if used for low-end products such as particleboard. If it's grown for high-end products such as specialty paper and fabrics, the value is even higher. There are already dozens of companies in the United States, Canada, and Europe making and selling clothes and accessories from hemp fabric. Many of these companies sell through the Internet, targeting young, hip buyers (see the list of web sites at the end of the book). Most North American hemp clothing is made from the hemp grown on government-licensed plots in Canada and Europe. Even with low acreages, high government involvement in the growing regions, and manufacturers' hassles surrounding transportation and border crossings, the clothes are competitively priced. They also look good and are tough. If hemp clothes were made with the same economies of scale enjoyed by big cotton mills, hemp would challenge cotton as the most popular natural fiber.

Can hemp compete with flax or cotton for fine textiles? Possibly, if the cost of processing the fiber into fine yarns can be kept lower in price. As a fiber, hemp is remarkably similar to flax, whose cloth, linen, has beautiful luster and wonderful texture, strength, absorbency, and dyeability.

Leftover hemp fiber can be pressed into plywood and particleboard, which may be up to twice as strong as wood particleboard and holds nails better.

PAPER

Hurds are the leftover fragments of the stems and stalk once all the fibers have been removed. As untreated and unrefined bits of plant mass, they can be used in a wide variety of products, from cement and insulation to paper. Hemp pulp can be ground and made into biodegradable plastics that can easily be broken down and/or recycled.

Hemp hurds make excellent, high-quality paper, but, to be economically feasible, the fiber needs to be grown near the paper mill. Most paper factories or mills can easily be converted to manufacture hemp paper as there's very little difference between wood pulp and hemp pulp. Trees contain approximately 60 percent cellulose while hemp contains about 77 percent. Hemp grows extremely quickly, generating more fiber per acre/year than forests. Hemp paper is longer lasting than wood–pulp paper, stronger, and acid-free. It is can also be made without chlorine, a chemical used in many pulp and paper mills with very negative effects on the environment and human health. Chlorine is estimated to cause up to 10 percent of all cancers. Hemp paper can be recycled seven times, wood-pulp paper only four times. Hemp paper lasts longer and, because of its low acidity, doesn't yellow or fox as much with age.

The first paper sheets (described in A.D. 105 in China by Ts'ai Lun) were made from hemp fiber. During the eighth century, the Chinese papermaking craftsmanship spread to the Muslim world. Baghdad became the center of papermaking in the Middle East; its small factories provided the paper used by generations of wonderfully talented Muslim artists and book illuminators. Europeans, who had, in the Middle Ages, used animal hides to make paper, switched to plant fiber when the invention and spread of the printing press in the 15th century caused an explosion of demand for paper. Rags were the main raw material until the early 19th century. People gathered and sold worn-out clothes made from hemp and flax and, more rarely, cotton. The fibers were cheap and were already softened and broken by wear. The Gutenberg Bible and the first drafts of the Declaration of Independence were printed on hemp paper. Important official documents were still printed on vellum, made of sheepskin, but the printed versions sold to the public or pasted up in public places were made of hemp paper. So was paper money, and the use of soft plant fibers still gives bills that appealing, distinctive feel.

The development of newspapers, mechanization of presses, and expansion of the reading public spurred demand for even cheaper sources of paper, as there simply weren't enough rags. This shortage threatened the monopoly for hemp and flax as papermaking fibers. New wood pulp-bleaching processes and the opening of the forests of North America solved the problems of the newspaper industry but deeply undercut the fine-paper market. Now only about 5 percent of the world's paper is made from annual plants like hemp, flax, cotton, sugarcane, bagasse, esparto, wheat straw, reeds, sisal, abaca, ananas, and other exotic species, but it is the most expensive and finest-quality writing material.

Hemp advocates say it's possible to leave the forests alone and go back to making paper from hemp. But is that really feasible? Technically, yes. Once plant cellulose is turned into pulp, it's pretty much all the same to the machinery of a paper mill.

Wisconsin, the largest paper-producing state in the United States, draws on its own forests and those of neighboring states, as well as Ontario, Canada, to feed its mills. The majority of paper produced from virgin fiber in Wisconsin is printing and writing paper, but the state is also a major manufacturer of household tissues, sanitary napkins, diapers, and industrial paper products. Wisconsin also has thousands of acres of agricultural land that's no longer farmed because of depressed commodity prices. Right now, underused farmland in Wisconsin could easily supply enough pulp for fine-paper production at the same price per ton as wood pulp.

The state has, according to local agricultural experts, one million acres available for growing hemp in a crop rotation plan. If mills in the state that make linerboard or packaging-grade paper switched to hemp, demand for hemp would likely exceed the production capacity of the land of Wisconsin farmers. The mills could simply draw on hemp production from neighboring states.

Recently, Dutch researchers looked at the feasibility of paper production from hemp. The three-year study involved scientists from 12 international institutes and cost US $10 million. The Dutch are searching for new crops that can be grown in rotation with their standard crops to control potato parasites and reduce the need for pesticides. The researchers found that hemp would be economically viable and developed a detailed business plan.

They recommended that 1,000 farmers from the Rhine Valley region of the Netherlands set up a cooperative, which would own shares in a new pulp factory. Additional funding would be needed from government subsidies and loans to meet start-up costs of US $32 million. After five years, the mill would be expanded, bringing the total investment to $75 million.

So far, no one has been willing to invest that much money, but a committee of farmers, government officials, and papermakers decided to continue researching and to start a small pilot project at a cost of $6 million.

INSULATION AND MORE

Raw hemp hurds can be coated with silica to make it moisture-repellent and then used as insulation or to replace the gravel mixed with cement. Cement made with hemp hurds is much lighter than regular cement, fireproof, flexible enough to be earthquake resistant, waterproof, and acts as a noise barrier. Hemp hurds treated with bitumen, a form of tar, make good floor insulation.

Hurds can be used as a soft and comfortable stuffing for mattresses, couches, and jackets. Hemp is as insulating as cotton, but, over time, does not clump together as cotton does. Hurds are also very absorbent and make excellent animal bedding and kitty litter.

Hemp hurds can also be used as an alternative to petroleum in plastics because of their naturally high level of cellulose. The hurds are crushed and beaten into a fine powder, then polymerized. Hemp plastic, which is recyclable and biodegradable, is already manufactured in Europe. As well, hemp oil can be used in most processes that now rely on petroleum.

COSMETICS AND SOAPS

Hemp oil makes a high-quality, economical base for cosmetics that use pure oil. Each hemp seed contains about 30 percent oil, which is extruded when the seeds are pressed.

Hemp oil is easily absorbed by the skin and, with its high content of nutrients, makes nourishing skin-care products. It's currently used as a base for lip gloss, makeup, hand lotions, shampoos, and soaps. Companies such as the Body Shop now sell hemp-based cosmetics and soaps.

If you prefer to make your own, try the following recipe for hemp soap, from Gail Cohen of Toronto, which makes five or six medium-sized bars:

HEMP SOAP

Molds (muffin tins, special soap molds, or any small glass or metal container)

1 lb (500 g)	melt-and-pour clear soap base (available at soap-supplies stores or online at www.soapscope.com, where I buy it).
1 tbsp (15 ml)	hemp oil (use clear oil so your soap won't have bits of residue or be really dark)
1 tsp (5 ml)	color, fragrance, or essential oils, if desired (green tea and lemongrass complement hemp oil).

1. Microwave soap base in a glass container, being careful not to let the soap base boil. Alternately, melt soap base in a double boiler or in a bowl over a pot of simmering water. Be sure you keep a lid on the bowl that is holding your soap; this will keep the moisture from evaporating from your soap base.
2. When the soap melts, add the hemp oil slowly, stirring gently to avoid creating bubbles. Add fragrance, color, or essential oils at this point and gently stir to combine.
3. Pour the soap slowly into the molds. Any bubbles may be removed by a spritz of rubbing alcohol.
4. Allow the soap to cool and harden for a couple of hours

undisturbed (depending on the size of the molds). If you must speed the drying time, place your soap in the freezer, being careful that the soap doesn't freeze. Once your soap has set, remove bars from their molds. Voila, they're ready to use. Because the soap is high in emollient vegetable glycerin, be sure to wrap your finished soaps in plastic wrap to keep them from drying out.

HEMP: AN ALTERNATIVE FUEL

Hemp oil and alcohol made from fermented plants are feasible alternatives to traditional energy, and could elimate the dependence of developed countries on imported crude oil. By using alcohol made from fermented hemp and diesel oil from pressed seeds, domestic oil reserves and other alternative fuels, we could become self-sufficient. Furthermore, many of the alternative fuels are cheaper to make.

The fuel of the future, according to Henry Ford and General Motors' scientist Charles F. Kettering, was ethyl alcohol made from farm products, and cellulose materials. Henry Ford's support for alternative fuel sources culminated in the Dearborn, Michigan, "Chemurgy" conferences in the 1930s. By then, alcohol-powered vehicles had been used in Europe for some 50 years, and, until oil prices dropped to near giveaway levels after World War II, ethyl alcohol was a serious contender as a major fuel source.

When Henry Ford told a *New York Times* reporter that ethyl alcohol was "the fuel of the future" in 1925, he expressed an opinion widely shared in the automotive industry. "The fuel of the future is going to come from fruit like that sumach out by the road, or from apples, weeds, sawdust—almost anything," he said. "There is fuel in every bit of vegetable matter that can be fermented. There's enough alcohol in one year's yield of an acre of potatoes to drive the machinery necessary to cultivate the fields for a hundred years." Ford wanted to open up new markets for American farmers, who were already faced with a crisis that would continue to worsen through the 1930s, and is back again: commodity prices that are, in real terms, as low as they were five centuries ago.

Three times in the past century, American farmers, business leaders, policy makers, and the public seemed ready to give alcohol fuels a chance; at the turn of the 20th century, as different types of cars went on the market; in the 1930s, with Henry Ford's blessing; and during the oil-price crunch of the 1970s and early 1980s. Each time, cheap gasoline undermined the alcohol industry. "Gasahol" development took off in Canada and the United States each time, and, in the 1980s, more than 100 corn-alcohol production plants were built in the United States and over one billion gallons of ethyl alcohol were sold per year for fuel. In Canada, some regional gasoline companies began selling gas-alcohol mixtures, which offer the anti-knock qualities of high octane fuel and prevent freezing of gas lines. Gasahol production was even an issue in the 1981 Ontario, Canada, provincial election, pushed by the opposition Liberals. However, oil and gas prices plunged in the late 1980s, not only stalling alcohol conversion but also hampering natural gas and hydrogen conversion.

Ethyl alcohol can replace gasoline in two ways: in modified internal combustion engines, and as an additive to gasoline in blends of 10 to 30 percent. It's not a new concept; "gasonol" was a blend of 20 percent sugar cane alcohol with gasoline and kerosene used in the Philippines in the 1930s. Koolmotor, Benzalcool, Moltaco, Lattybentyl, Natelite, Alcool, and Agrol were alcohol-gasoline fuels sold in Britain, Italy, Hungary, Sweden, South Africa, Brazil, and the U.S. in the 1920s and 1930s.

Alcohol was an important fuel before the invention of the car. In the first half of the 19th century, before petroleum was discovered in Ontario and Ohio, the leading fuel was "camphene" (sometimes simply called "burning fluid"). It was a blend of high-proof ethyl alcohol with 20 to 50 percent turpentine to color the flame and a few drops of camphor oil to mask the turpentine smell. Alcohol for camphene was an important mainstay for distilleries, and many sold between one-third and 80 percent of their product on the fuel market.

In the 1830s, various alcohol blends, which were much cleaner, had replaced increasingly expensive whale oil in most parts of the United States. In the 1850s, camphene (at $.50 per gallon) was cheaper than whale oil ($1.30 to $2.50 per gallon) and lard oil (90 cents per gallon). The Canadian invention, kerosene, came on the market at the same time. It was made from coal oil and cost about the same as alcohol, with the added benefit that it was not nearly as volatile.

Alcohol might have kept a hefty share of the market, but a $2.08-a-gallon tax imposed on beverage alcohol during the Civil War also applied to industrial alcohol and effectively killed the lamp alcohol business. In Europe, where there was no such tax, alcohol was a ready fuel when the internal combustion engine was developed.

Samuel Morey developed the first internal combustion engine in the United States in the 1820s. It ran on ethyl alcohol and turpentine and powered an experimental wagon and a small boat at eight miles (12.8 kilometers) per hour up the Connecticut River. However, potential financial backers kept their money in steamships and railways, and Morey's invention stayed on the shelf. In the 1860s German inventor Nicholas August Otto developed an internal combustion engine that used vaporized alcohol, but he could not get a patent from the Kingdom of Prussia. American inventor George Brayton developed an engine in the 1870s, but used gasoline, a petroleum by-product that was cheap because no one had yet found a use for the dangerously volatile fluid.

In Europe, where all petroleum products were relatively expensive, work on alcohol motors continued. Thirty percent of the locomotive engines produced by the Otto Gas Engine Works in Germany ran on alcohol. One-third of the heavy locomotives produced at the Deutz Gas engine works of Germany ran on pure ethyl alcohol, and much of the World War I German military equipment used alcohol for fuel. When oil shortages seemed likely to paralyze Germany's transportation system in 1915, thousands of engines were quickly modified. "Every motor car in the empire was adapted to run on alcohol. It is possible that Germany would have been beaten already [by 1917] if production of alcohol had not formed an important part of the agricultural economy," Irish historian George Tweedy later wrote. A representative of the Detroit Board of Commerce, James S. Capen, told the Senate Finance Committee that alcohol was "preferable" to gasoline because it was safer, "absolutely clean and sanitary," and because "artificial shortages" could not raise the price in the future. Pure alcohol fuel went on sale in Peoria, Illinois, at 32 cents per gallon in January 1907 as the tax took effect, and prices elsewhere in the States hovered around 25 to 30 cents. At the same time, gasoline prices of 18 to 22 cents per gallon were beginning to drop as new Texas oil fields came on line and found markets on the East Coast.

In Germany in 1926, a commercial fuel called Monopolin was introduced and "favorably recieved due to its anti-knock qualities." The fuel, which included I. G. Farben's octane-boosting iron carbonyl additive, was endorsed by a famous race car driver of the era, Herbert Ernst, and alcohol use in fuel climbed from 250,000 gallons in 1923 to 46 million gallons in 1932. In 1930 gasoline importers were required to buy from 2.5 to 6 percent alcohol relative to their gasoline import volumes to use in blends. In 1933, I. G. Farben and several oil companies acquired 51 percent of Monopolin. Production of alcohol did not diminish but by 1937 had climbed to about 52 million gallons per year as part of Hitler's war preparations.

The total use of alcohol as a substitute fuel in Europe may have never exceeded 5 percent, according to the American Petroleum Institute. Synthetic gasoline and benzene created by I. G. Farben from coal substituted for 7 percent and 6.5 percent respectively of European petroleum by 1937. Synthetic gasoline was cheaper (at 17 to 19 cents per gallon) than alcohol at around 25 cents per gallon, API says. By 1937 motorists from Indiana to South Dakota were urged to use Agrol, an ethyl alcohol blend with gasoline. Two types were available—Agrol 5, with 5 to 7 percent alcohol, and Agrol 10, with 12.5 to 17 percent alcohol. "Try a tankful—you'll be thankful," the Agrol brochures said. The blend was sold to high initial enthusiasm at 2,000 service stations.

Nevertheless, by 1939, the Atchison Agrol plant closed its doors, lacking viable markets. The experiment had failed, but that was not the end of the story. As the U.S. declared war two years later, the California assembly considered a motion to create an auxiliary fuel from surplus fruits and vegetables. President Franklin Roosevelt wrote the speaker of the assembly and said:

> *While it is true that a number of foreign countries process agricultural materials for the production of alcohol as a motor fuel, it is equally true that the motor fuel economy of countries possessing no petroleum resources is very different from such economy in the United States. It has never been established in this country that the conversion of agricultural products into motor fuel is economically feasible or necessary for national defense. On the other hand, it has been recognized for a long time that a real need exists in this country for the development of all the information possible on this very contentious subject...*

Roosevelt's intense political feud with the Republican forces who backed chemurgy in the 1930s led him to oppose virtually anything that the Midwestern Republicans advanced, but Roosevelt's judgment was premature and wrong.

Editorials by Lowell Thomas and other radio announcers paid for by oil industry sponsors claimed that alcohol fuel would make "speakeasys" out of gasoline stations because bootleggers could easily separate out the gasoline and sell the alcohol. Thomas said: "The automobile manufacturer resents it [alcohol] because it interferes with the horsepower of the motorist's car, requires extensive carburetor changes and presents other diffi-culties…" (In fact, this might be true of pure alcohol but not alcohol blends with gasoline). Thomas's radio address was recorded in a cable sent from Sun Oil Co.'s J. Howard Pew to H. D. Collier, president of Standard Oil Co. of California, on April 26, 1933.

In its 1980 revival, gasohol never got far enough to worry the oil companies. A few added small amounts of alcohol to gasoline and pocketed windfall profits, since alcohol was not hit by the excise taxes that governments pile onto gasoline. Still, alterna-tive energy advocates could not compete with the clout of oil companies. The corporations hire the best lobbyists and give generously to political parties. Former oil executives hold key positions in Washington. But governments have another reason to keep the petroleum flowing. Tax revenues — almost always a percentage of the pump price — rise with every price increase. It costs less than 60 cents a barrel to extract a barrel of oil from the deserts of Kuwait and get it onto a supertanker. Every cent made on top of that goes to people with a vested interest in maintain-ing the status quo: producing countries, supertanker and pipeline owners, oil companies, refiners, and governments. The military gets money to protect this traffic; everyone gets a piece of the action except the consumer.

The cost to the environment from oil-field pollution, pipeline leaks, tanker wrecks, refinery effluent, and air pollution, are rarely factored in.

Hemp oil and gasohol advocates have come up with some very creative ways to drive home the message that the West does not need to be held hostage by the repressive and often hostile regimes that control the bulk of the world's fossil fuel.

In 2000, Grayson Sigler and Kellie Ogilvie created the Hempcar to show the American public an alternative. After a 10,000-mile (16,000-kilometer) journey around the continent beginning in Washington, D.C., on July 4, 2001, they took the car to Japan. "If hemp were legal to grow in the U.S., technologies such as pyrolysis would make hemp fuels economically competitive with petrol fuels," says Sigler. "The emissions associated with the use of hemp fuels are far less toxic than for fossil fuels, and hemp helps slow down global warming by absorbing CO_2 from the air while it is growing.

The Hemp car, which has traveled through North America powered by hemp products, raises awareness of the plant.

Pyrolysis is the thermochemical process that converts organic materials into usable fuels with high fuel-to-feed ratios, making it the most efficient process for biomass conversion, and the method most capable of competing with and eventually replacing nonrenewable fossil fuel resources. Chemical decomposition through pyrolysis is the same technology used to refine crude fossil fuel oil and coal. Pyrolysis of wood to produce charcoal was a major industry in the 1800s, supplying the fuel for the Industrial Revolution, until charcoal was replaced by coal.

So, can we look forward to filling up our tanks with hemp oil? "Not in the next decade," Sigler told news reporters when he began his voyage. "Prohibition has made hemp oil quite expensive, and the glut of petroleum fuels exacerbates the problem."

Recently Joshua and Kaia Tickell built the "Veggie Van," a fryer-grease-powered Winnebago that logged over 25,000 miles (40,200 kilometers) promoting the "biodiesel" concept in the

U.S. It could just as easily run on hemp seed oil, either directly from seed presses or after it's been used for frying.

Biodiesel is the name for a variety of ester-based oxygenated fuels made from hemp oil, other vegetable oils, or animal fats. The concept of using vegetable oil as an engine fuel dates back to 1895 when Dr. Rudolf Diesel developed the first diesel engine to run on vegetable oil. Diesel demonstrated his engine at the World Exhibition in Paris in 1900, using peanut oil as fuel.

Because it has properties similar to petroleum diesel fuel, biodiesel can be blended in any ratio with petroleum diesel fuel. In fact, many federal and state fleet vehicles are already using biodiesel blends in their existing diesel engines.

The low emissions of biodiesel make it an ideal fuel for use in marine areas, national parks and forests, and heavily polluted cities. Biodiesel has many advantages as a transport fuel. For example, it can be produced from domestically grown oilseed plants such as hemp.

When burned in a diesel engine, biodiesel replaces the exhaust odor of petroleum diesel with the pleasant smell of hemp, popcorn, or French fries.

The industrial world currently runs on fossil fuel: natural gas, oil, and coal. Fossil fuel resources are nonrenewable and contain varying levels of sulfur, which is the source of many of the environmental pollution problems threatening much of the world.

Removing sulfur compounds from fossil fuels is a major expense to the energy producers. Fossil-plant carbon — coal — is one of Earth's ways of storing carbon dioxide. When coal is burned, this carbon dioxide is added to the Earth's atmosphere. And, since many of the world's forests are being cleared, nature has no way to lock the CO_2 away — it's added to the brew of greenhouse gases.

It is likely that peak oil and gas production in the United States has been reached. The oil fields of Texas, Oklahoma, and Ohio are being pumped at their capacity, and the only major oil fields that are undeveloped are in environmentally-sensitive parts of the continental shelf and Alaska. The situation for recoverable coal, worldwide, is more favorable. Peak production is estimated to happen shortly after 2100. The costs of environmental pollution and destruction associated with coal-fired industries are simply too high: acid rain, smog, greenhouse gases, and strip-mined land.

Even if the pollution problems of fossil fuel use are solved, the financial costs of this form of energy will still rise because of the dwindling availability of this nonrenewable world resource, but the dollar cost of energy production from biomass conversion will remain relatively constant because the world biomass resource is renewable on a yearly basis.

However, the automobile industry is hooked on cheap gasoline. Oil companies are in the business of taking fuel from the ground, not squeezing it from seeds or distilling it from fermented plants. U.S. foreign policy is geared to ensuring "stability" in regions that are prepared to guarantee a steady flow of relatively cheap energy.

In 1979, Stanford Research Institute conducted a Mission Analysis study for the U.S. Department of Energy. The scientists chose five types of biomass materials to investigate for energy conversion: woody plants, herbaceous plants (those that do not produce persistent woody material), aquatic plants, and manure. Herbaceous plants were divided into two categories: those with low moisture content and those with high moisture content.

Biomass conversion may be conducted on two broad pathways: chemical decomposition and biological digestion.

Chemical decomposition can be utilized for energy conversion of all five categories of biomass materials, but low-moisture herbaceous (small grain field residues) and woody (wood industry wastes, and standing vegetation not suitable for lumber) are the most suitable.

Biological processes are essentially microbic digestion and

fermentation. High-moisture herbaceous plants (vegetables, sugarcane, sugar beet, corn, sorghum, cotton), marine crops, and manure are most suitable for biological digestion.

Anaerobic digestion produces high and intermediate BTU gases. (High-BTU gas is methane; intermediate-BTU gas comprises methane mixed with carbon monoxide and carbon dioxide.) Methane can be efficiently converted into methanol, which can be used as a propane or natural gas replacement.

Fermentation produces ethyl and other alcohols, but the process is too costly in terms of cultivated land use and too inefficient in terms of alcohol production to feasibly supply enough fuel alcohol to power industrial society.

To be most efficient, farmers should be encouraged to grow energy crops capable of producing 10 tons per acre in 90 to 120 days. The crop would have to be naturally high in cellulose, grow in almost all climactic zones in the United States, and not compete with food production for the most fertile land. Since hemp grows well on marginal soil, it could be grown in rotation with food crops or on marginal land where other crop production isn't profitable.

So why don't we have methanol at the filling station? The scientists said the problem was government certification under the *Clean Air Act* that required automobile manufacturers to meet standards set by the EPA based on fuels available on a national level. Since methanol fuel standards had not been set, the car makers couldn't make the new fleet until the methanol fuel was available at the pump. This catch-22 situation continues today. Government is unwilling to subsidize pilot energy farms and biomass refinery construction because fossil fuel producers control the energy industry. The danger of the reliance on fossil fuels is obvious: economic uncertainty from fluctuating prices; political instability and war in the Middle East; environmental damage from oil fields, refineries, and oil tanker spills.

And, as the United States goes, so does Canada, Europe, and the rest of the developed world.

Governments still toy with the idea of gasoline substitutes. On June 12, 1989, during his losing run for re-election, President George Bush Sr. unveiled an ambitious plan to reduce smog in Southern California and the rest of the United States' most populous cities and to reduce acid rain pollution. Bush suggested car makers be required to make methanol-powered cars for use in nine urban areas plagued by air pollution, calling methanol "home-grown energy for America."

William Reilly, then chief of the Environmental Protection Agency, estimated the cost of the plan would be between $14 billion and $19 billion a year. Bush said, "Too many Americans continue to breathe dirty air, and political paralysis has plagued further progress against air pollution. We've seen enough of this stalemate. It's time to clear the air." But, when Bush lost the election, the idea was not picked up by President Bill Clinton, nor has it been revived by George W. Bush, despite the troubles in the Middle East.

Biomass and seed oil fuel advocates say the energy needs of the United States—by far the world's largest consumer of fossil fuels—could be met by farming about 6 percent of the landmass of the lower 48 states. This production would not add any net carbon dioxide to the atmosphere. The best biomass producer per acre, on prime or marginal farmland, is probably hemp.

MEDICAL USES

Jesus Christ and his apostles may have used a cannabis-based anointing oil to help cure people with crippling diseases. Researchers in the United States say the oil used in the early days of the Christian church contained a cannabis extract called *kaneh-bosem*. They claim the extract, which is absorbed into the body when placed on the skin, could have helped cure people with a variety of physical and mental problems. Chris Bennett, author of an article printed in *High Times* and carried in media around the world, says his findings are based on a study of scriptural texts. Bennett says he isn't questioning the validity of New Testament miracles or the power of faith. He just wants an examination of the medical substances that were used at the time of Christ, including cannabis. In fact, it was an old medication in southern and western Asia when the New Testament was written. Its use is mentioned in ancient texts and archaeological records.

"The holy anointing oil, as described in the original Hebrew version of the recipe in Exodus, contained over six pounds of *keneh-bosum* — a substance identified by respected etymology, linguists, anthropologists, botanists and other researchers as cannabis extracted into about six quarts of olive oil along with a variety of other fragrant herbs," Bennett says.

The ancient anointed ones were literally drenched in this potent mixture. In the ancient world, diseases such as epilepsy were attributed to demonic possession. To cure somebody of such an illness, even with the aid of certain herbs, was considered exorcism or miraculous healing. Interestingly, cannabis has been shown to be effective in the treatment of not only epilepsy but many of the other ailments that Jesus and the disciples healed people of such as skin diseases, eye problems and menstrual problems...If cannabis was one of the main ingredients of the ancient Christian anointing oil, as history indicates, and receiving this oil is what made Jesus the Christ and his followers Christians, then persecuting those who use cannabis could be considered anti-Christ.

Fundamentalist Christians were not thrilled with this theory. In a response to the article published on JesusJournal.com, critics said: "As many of us know firsthand, Jesus often becomes the final hope for the pharmacologically impaired." And John Cunyus, the author of *A Handbook for Christian*

Healing, brought some wit to the debate when he said that "the Bible does say that St. Stephen was stoned...but perhaps not in that sense!"

That debate will continue for some time, as will the fight over medicinal marijuana.

David Solomon, in his foreword to his 1966 collection of scientific articles, published as *The Marihuana Papers*, argues:

Marihuana should be accorded the medical status it once had in this country as a legitimate prescription item. After 1937, with the passage of the Marihuana Tax Act *and subsequent federal and state legislation, it became virtually impossible for physicians to obtain or prescribe marihuana preparations for their patients. Thus, the medical profession was denied access to a versatile pharmaceutical tool with a history of therapeutic utility going back thousands of years"*

Of course, he wasn't the first person to advocate medical marijuana. Shen-Nung, writing in China 5,000 years ago, prescribed cannabis for beri-beri, constipation, "female weakness," gout, malaria, rheumatism, and absentmindedness. In Egypt in 2000 B.C., cannabis was a good treatment for sore eyes. And it was that use that would reopen the debate on medical pot some 4,000 years later.

"To the agriculturist, cannabis is a fiber crop; to the physician, it is an enigma; to the user, a euphoriant; to the police, a menace; to the trafficker, a source of profitable danger; to the convict or parolee and his family, a source of sorrow," medical marijuana activist Dr. Tod Mikuriya says. And, in medicine, as in so many other ways, cannabis has been held in high and low esteem at various times throughout recorded history. These days, among a growing number of people, medicinal marijuana is making a comeback.

Since 1996, eight U.S. states (Alaska, California, Colorado, Hawaii, Maine, Nevada, Oregon, and Washington) and the fed-

eral government of Canada have enacted laws or passed refer-
enda that effectively allow patients to use medical marijuana on
the advice of their physicians. As well, Arizona passed legislation
to allow physicians to write prescriptions for medical marijuana
use. There's always one catch. Despite public and legislative
support in these places, medicinal marijuana has not been particularly easy to come by, especially from government-approved
sources. Quite simply, there aren't any in North America. People
end up having to grow their own or buy cannabis. Either way,
they break the law.

Cannabis has been a medicine for as long as it's been a recreational drug and is still used extensively in the Ayruvedic,
Unani, and Tibbi systems of medicine of the Indian subcontinent. Two preparations of cannabis, a liquid extract and a
tincture, are listed in the 1954 and 1966 *Pharmacopoeias of India,*
published with the blessing of the country's medical establish-
ment. The texts tell how to make and use the extracts, which
work as a sedative, hypnotic, analgesic, antispasmodic, and anti-
hemorrhoid medication.

Until relatively recently, cannabis also had a place in
European medicine. In ancient Greece, a culture that didn't use
it as a recreational drug, cannabis was relied on as a remedy for
earache, edema, and inflammation. Various other uses, in a
number of European regions, included the treatment of tetanus,
hydrophobia (rabies), delirium tremens, infantile convulsions,
neuralgia and other nervous disorders, cholera, menorrhagia,
rheumatism, hay fever, asthma, skin diseases, and protracted
labor during childbirth.

Several years after the return of Napoleon's army from
Egypt, cannabis became widely accepted by Western medical
practitioners. Although previously it had had limited use for
such purposes as the treatment of burns, the scientific members
of Napoleon's forces were interested in the drug's pain-relieving
and sedative effects. Doctors experimented with it during

Napoleon's reign and, to a greater extent, following his rule. By the 1840s, the work of such physicians as W. B. O'Shaughnessy, Louis Aubert-Roche, and Jacques-Joseph Moreau de Tours drew wide attention to this drug.

Just before the beginning of the U.S. Civil War, American doctors began discussing the medical uses of cannabis. In 1860, a Committee on Cannabis Indica of the Ohio State Medical Society was convened. It reviewed two scientific reports, the first by W. B. O'Shaughnessy in 1839, and the second by Queen Victoria's physician, Russell Reynolds. Both doctors recommended cannabis's medical use for a variety of ailments and as a mild euphoriant. At that time, cannabis had wide support among the medical community. It was available without a prescription and was used in many patent medicines.

Cannabis use in medicine was supplanted in the early years of the 20th century, and, with the ban on marijuana and hemp, it was effectively driven from the Western pharmacopoeia. Studies by Congress, the City of New York, and the Nixon administration ignored the medical benefits of marijuana. In 1970, when the Canadian government set up an expert study on the use of marijuana, cannabis had been outlawed for nearly two generations. Members of the commission, who were generally sympathetic to the idea of decriminalization, could no longer find reputable physicians prepared to vouch for cannabis. However, this would change over the next decade.

In 1972, American researchers found that cannabis reduced intraocular pressure—the pressure of fluid in the eye. It was found that as the dose of marijuana increased, the pressure within the eye decreased by up to 30 percent. This occurred in healthy people as well as in those with glaucoma, a disease of the eye in which increased intraocular pressure causes intense pain and may lead to blindness. Very quickly, many people with glaucoma, even those who had never used marijuana before, tried it as a way of controlling their condition and reversing some of the disease's effects. Since then, medical cannabis research and use has focused on glaucoma and the following conditions:

- Cancer: As an aid to chemotherapy, which often has side effects of nausea, vomiting, and loss of appetite. Marijuana helps offset some of these effects, and is especially useful for increasing appetite.
- Multiple sclerosis (MS): MS causes the destruction of patches of myelin in the brain and spinal cord. Victims eventually cannot walk or sit up, and become crippled and bedridden — often with terrible muscle spasms. Medications that provide some relief from these spasms are addictive. Marijuana reduces spasms in patients with MS.
- AIDS: AZT and other drugs used to treat AIDS result in nausea and anorexia. Like chemotherapy in cancer patients, this often causes severe weight loss, which impairs the body's ability to fight the disease. Marijuana helps reduce nausea and increases the appetite.
- Pain relief: Animal tests show cannabinoids are analgesic and reduce neuropathic pain. Supporters of medical marijuana say there's likely similar action in humans. Opponents of cannabis use say studies show that cannabinoids are no more effective than codeine and have enough side effects to limit their use.

In recent studies, the anti-nausea and anti-vomiting effects of delta-9-tetrahydrocannabinol (THC) in children receiving cancer chemotherapy were compared with those of metoclopramide syrup and prochlorperazine tablets in two double-blind studies. THC was found to be a significantly better anti-nausea and anti-vomiting agent, but not all patients obtained relief of nausea and vomiting with THC. In some patients, THC enhanced appetite during a course of chemotherapy.

Numerous published studies (see sources list at the end of the book) suggest that marijuana has medical value in treating patients with serious illnesses such as AIDS, glaucoma, cancer, multiple sclerosis, epilepsy, and chronic pain. In 1999, the Institute of Medicine, in the most comprehensive study of medical marijuana's efficacy, concluded that, "Nausea, appetite loss, pain and anxiety...all can be mitigated by marijuana."

Allowing patients legal access to medical marijuana has been discussed by numerous organizations, including the AIDS Action Council, American Bar Association, American Public Health Association, California Medical Association, National Association of Attorneys General, and several state nurses' associations.

Public opinion is also in favor of ending the prohibition of medical marijuana. According to a 1999 Gallup poll, 73 percent of Americans are in favor of "making marijuana legally available for doctors to prescribe in order to reduce pain and suffering." That support has manifested itself at the ballot box: since 1996, when California voters endorsed Proposition 215, electors in seven states and the District of Columbia have passed favorable medical marijuana ballot initiatives.

Currently, laws that effectively remove state-level criminal penalties for possessing medical marijuana are in place in Alaska, California, Colorado, Hawaii, Maine, Nevada, Oregon, and Washington. Ten states have symbolic medical marijuana laws (laws that support medical marijuana but do not provide patients with legal protection under state law). In 1998, voters in the District of Columbia approved their medical marijuana initiative by 69 percent, but Congress has nullified the election results, preventing the will of the voters from taking effect. (Congress can nullify the medical marijuana law in the District of Columbia because the region is a federal district and not a state.)

There has been a federal backlash. In 1998, the House of Representatives voted 311–94 for a nonbinding resolution condemning medical marijuana. In 1978, the federal government had been forced to allow some patients access to medical marijuana after the courts recognized a "medical necessity" defense, and the Investigational New Drug (IND) compassionate access program was created. The IND, which allowed some patients to receive medical marijuana from the government, stopped taking applications for medicinal marijuana in 1992 after it was flooded by applications from AIDS patients who had read recent reports that marijuana relieved some of the symptoms of the disease. However, as of mid-2002, it was still supplying medical marijuana to eight patients.

The U.S. federal government, unlike its counterparts in Canada and Europe, is vehemently opposed to medicinal marijuana use and gives large amounts of money to academic research that attempts to prove marijuana is an ineffective treatment. The government has threatened to withhold federal grants from any state that begins a program to supply patients with the drug.

In addition to changing state laws, medical marijuana advocates have also pursued reform through the courts. Marijuana is classified as a Schedule I substance, defined as having a high potential for abuse and no medicinal value. In 1972, a petition was submitted to the Bureau of Narcotics and Dangerous Drugs (now known as the Drug Enforcement Administration, or DEA) to reschedule marijuana so that it could be prescribed to patients. In 1988, the DEA's chief administrative law judge, Francis L. Young, ruled that, "Marijuana, in its natural form, is one of the safest therapeutically active substances known...It would be unreasonable, arbitrary and capricious for DEA to continue to stand between those sufferers and the benefits of this substance..." The DEA refused to implement this ruling and continues to classify marijuana as a Schedule I substance.

In 1997, *Conant v. McCaffrey*, a class-action lawsuit, was filed on behalf of physicians and seriously ill patients against Bill Clinton's "Drug Czar" General Barry McCaffrey and other top federal officials who threatened to revoke prescription licenses or criminally prosecute physicians who recommend medical marijuana. The lawsuit argued that "physicians and patients have the right, protected by the First Amendment to the U.S. Constitution, to communicate in the context of a bona fide physician-patient relationship, without government interference or threats of punishment, about the potential benefits and risks of the medical use of marijuana." In 2000, U.S. District Court Judge William Alsup enjoined the federal government to not penalize doctors who recommend marijuana by revoking their licenses to dispense medication.

In another case, *U.S. v. Oakland Cannabis Buyers' Cooperative,* the federal government challenged the ability of medical marijuana distribution centers to provide patients with marijuana. In 1999, the Ninth U.S. Circuit Court of Appeals ruled 3–0 that "medical necessity" is a valid defense against federal marijuana distribution charges if a distributor can prove that the patients it serves are seriously ill, face imminent harm without marijuana, and have no effective legal alternatives.

The U.S. Supreme Court issued an "emergency" order at the Clinton Administration's request, temporarily barring the Oakland Cannabis Buyers' Cooperative from distributing medical marijuana. The Supreme Court heard the case in the spring of 2001, and decided against the Oakland group. The court unanimously ruled that medical use of marijuana is not a valid exception to the federal law that classifies marijuana as an illegal substance.

In his decision for the court, Justice Clarence Thomas wrote that the controlled substance statute "includes no exception at all for any medical use of marijuana." Although voting with the majority, three justices (John Paul Stevens, David Souter, and Ruth Bader Ginsburg) wrote a concurring opinion stating that the decision went too far. They believe that there should have been a medical-necessity option for a patient "for whom there is no alternative means of avoiding starvation or extraordinary suffering."

Dr. Molly Fry and her husband, El Dorado County district attorney candidate Dale Schafer, were the first to be raided after the decision. When their medical and legal consultation business, the California Medical Research Center, was searched in late September 2001 and again in early October after DEA agents infiltrated a grow seminar with forged recommendations. Police seized about 7,000 patient records, along with computers and 32 plants that Dr. Fry kept for personal use in her battle against breast cancer. Her 14-year-old son was kept handcuffed for hours while police searched the Fry-Schafer home.

The Ventura County home of Lynn and Judy Osburn, suppliers for the Los Angeles Cannabis Resource Center, was raided a few days later. More than 200 plants were seized. Dr. Bill Eidelman, a doctor who supports medical marijuana, was next. San Bernardino County narcotics officers raided his Santa Monica offices and seized over 5,000 patient records. Then, on October 25, the Los Angeles Cannabis Resource Center in West Hollywood was raided by 30 DEA agents. Approximately 400 plants, 3,000 records, lights, equipment, and computers were taken away, despite the vehement protests of the city council and sheriff's department officials, who supported the work that the LACRC has done since Proposition 215 passed in 1996. The California medical marijuana movement wasn't dealt a deathblow, but it's now burdened with huge legal fees and court battles. Patients are worried, and many of them have stopped using medical pot. In San Francisco, buyers' clubs were put under noticeably increased surveillance, and activists say hydroponic-supply shops were approached by federal agents hoping to gain cooperation in impending busts.

So patients find themselves in a catch-22. In states where medicinal marijuana has public support and the blessing of the legislature, medicinal marijuana is unavailable and police are aggressively hunting down people who are willing to take the risk of supplying it.

In Canada, medical marijuana is legal, and, in the late 1990s, the government actually took steps to grow it for those people with prescriptions. Then health minister Allan Rock invited reporters to see the government's grow operation. Canada's government grows medicinal marijuana in a hydroponic lab deep in a mine in Flin Flon, a small town in northern Manitoba. The pot mine resembles a set in an old James Bond movie, and its product is considered such a public menace that visits to the marijuana mine are strictly limited. Special regulations allow patients with conditions such as AIDS and back pain to use the illegal drug to treat their symptoms. Officials with former health minister Allan Rock said in 2001 that marijuana from the mine would be in those patients' hands within weeks.

Four months later, more than 550 pounds (250 kilograms) of the federally sanctioned buds were harvested. For months, they sat in a secure cold storage grotto, 1,100 feet (360 meters) underground. Entrances to the storage facility were video-monitored constantly by the Royal Canadian Mounted Police, who could arrive quickly enough to capture any ambitious thieves. At the time of the first harvest, 798 people were approved to possess marijuana as medicine, but only 106 of them had permission either to grow the drug themselves or to have someone else grow it for them. The rest had to wait for the marijuana from the subarctic mine, but, because it was grown from batches of seeds seized by police, it was too inconsistent to prescribe.

At the same time, both the Canadian Medical Association and the Canadian Medical Protective Association told physicians not to sign patients' requests to be federally approved to possess cannabis. "The objective is not to prevent them from having access to something that may relieve their symptoms, but to protect them against an unproven treatment," CMA president Henry Haddad said. The agencies were supported by new Canadian Health Minister Anne McLellan, a social conservative from Alberta, who said the government pot would be given only to people enrolled in clinical trials. The rest of the people with marijuana prescriptions would, presumably, have to buy their drug from street dealers or illegally grow their own. The government had buckled under pressure from the U.S. government and the powerful medical/pharmaceutical lobby.

Ted Smith, founder of the Victoria-based Cannabis Buyers' Clubs of Canada, which, despite the legal risk, grows and delivers marijuana as medicine to 950 members. Smith said few people are bothering to apply for marijuana from the government's $5.8 million pot-in-the-mine program anymore, and the whole project is still up in the air. Rock would have gone ahead, but McLellan has sent the issue back to her department for "more studies." Smith doesn't believe McLellan, or any other politician, will be able to resist the pressure of the antimarijuana lobbies. "The only way things will happen here is by constant, passive, civil disobedience," says Smith, who, in 2002, faced six marijuana-related charges. "Most people are giving up on [the Canadian health department]. They figure, why fill out all this paperwork? Doctors have been told not to sign it for them and then there's nowhere to get it, so what's the point?"

While North American politicians continue to dither over medicinal marijuana or ban it altogether, research continues. A British drug company, G.W. Pharmaceuticals, is producing a cannabis aerosol spray under license to the U.K. government. Similar to a breath spray, it seems to offer the medical benefits of marijuana without the harmful side effects of smoking. The company has been testing the spray in clinical trials over the past five years in Britain and Europe with 400 people who have multiple sclerosis, cancer, rheumatoid arthritis, and spinal-cord injuries. However, when the company offered the spray to Canada's health department for clinical trials, the offer was declined. Medicinal marijuana advocates believe the government is afraid the aerosol spray would kill one of the arguments of the medical community, that smoking pot is dangerous because the smoke contains tars.

Still, G.W. Pharmaceuticals has applied to have use of the spray approved under Britain's regulatory regime for prescription drugs. Its target is to have the spray on the market in early 2004. Then it plans to apply to U.S. and Canadian regulators for approval as a prescription drug and appeal to the courts if regulators don't give the product a fair hearing.

CHAPTER 3

Defying the DEA:
The Fight for Cannabis

On Valentine's Day 2002, Ken Hayes, a wanted man in America, boarded a ferry at Horseshoe Bay bound for British Columbia's Sunshine Coast. Hayes, one of America's most outspoken advocates of medical marijuana, became one of thousands of "refugees" from the War on Drugs who have left the U.S. rather than face the wrath of the Bush administration.

In 2001 Hayes won a well-publicized victory in Sonoma County, California, when he was acquitted of marijuana trafficking charges. He mounted a medical defense, which has been successful in California's North Coast counties, where voters strongly supported Proposition 215, the 1996 initiative that allowed pot use with a doctor's recommendation. The day he was acquitted, DEA agents started investigating Hayes and the San Francisco marijuana buyers' club he co-owned. When an anonymous caller tipped Hayes to the investigation in January 2002, he fled north to Canada with his girlfriend and 3-year-old daughter. As he drove through Washington, U.S. prosecutors charged him with being a "large-scale" drug trafficker, a crime which carries a possible sentence of 10 years to life.

Hayes wasn't the first Drug War refugee. Steve Tuck, a disabled Army veteran who is wanted in Humboldt County, California, on six felony pot charges; Steve Kubby, a former California Libertarian Party gubernatorial candidate, who is battling Placer County drug charges and is campaigning for medical marijuana rights; and Renee Boje, a 32-year-old graphic artist from Santa Monica, who is fighting extradition to the United States on marijuana-related charges, have moved to Canada in the past few years. All live on the Sunshine Coast, a long strip of land north of Vancouver accessible only by ferry or seaplane. Vancouver, Canada's third-largest city, is home to the country's largest pot club, the British Columbia Compassion Society, and at least 60 Americans are registered members of medical pot dispensaries in the province.

The British Columbia Compassion Society, with 1,600 members, operates openly a block away from a neighborhood police storefront, selling 10 oz (300 grams) of pot daily, and mailing packages of pot to customers throughout Canada. Canadian courts have ruled that prosecuting people for possession of small amounts of marijuana violates their civil rights, but, fearful of bad press and a backlash in the marijuana-friendly city, police had already decided to leave the Compassion Society alone.

Protesters in Sydney, Australia, against the country's marijuana ban by carrying a giant joint.

During the 1960s and early '70s, tens of thousands of Americans moved north to avoid the Vietnam War. Many of them stayed, even after a blanket pardon was issued to draft dodgers and deserters by President Jimmy Carter. Now, a new generation of antiwar refugees are coming to Canada, this time to escape the worst excesses of the failed War on Drugs.

Most are settling on Canada's Pacific Coast, in the cedar rain forests and rugged islands of British Columbia. The province is a place of gentle climate and rough politics, a place where conservative loggers and miners live side by side and in relative peace with aging hippies, pot growers, artists, and urban refugees.

British Columbia's economy took a major hit when, in 2001, the Bush administration placed a heavy duty on softwood lumber. But that decision has probably been a spur to B.C.'s new major farming crop: pot. It's worth at least $1.5 billion a year.

For two generations, botanists in B.C. and Ontario (many of them draft dodgers from the States who came up to Canada during the Vietnam War) have been designing better marijuana plants. Plants of the new breed—smaller, with spreading crowns of flower tops—bear little resemblance to the six-foot (two-meter) plants that amateur growers cultivated when North Americans started planting acreages of pot in the 1960s.

Flower tops are about five times more potent than ordinary

Mexican street marijuana (30 to 35 percent to six percent, respectively). In fact, B.C. Bud, as it's known, is about as strong as the hashish that was on the streets 25 years ago.

One B.C.-based botanist and pot grower advocates cloning pot plants, rather than growing them from seed, because the clones are perfect reproductions of the parent plant. "Marijuana is one of the easiest plants to clone," he says: a single plant can produce up to 1½ pounds (0.7 kilograms) of smokable substance in a relatively short cultivation period. At that rate, a low-end grower with only 25 plants can earn up to $100,000 a year.

Growing styles have changed too. Rather than planting acres of hemp, growers now cultivate small patches scattered throughout wilderness areas. Thieves who find some of the small plots don't get the entire crop. If the police find a little patch and manage to trace it to the grower, the marijuana grower may be able to convince a judge that the plants were for personal use, rather than for sale. That can be the difference between probation and jail. Growers are prepared for a certain amount of loss. One B.C. grower says: "One for the thieves, one for the cops, and one for me." B.C. isn't the only place where pot growers are busy. In 2000 police executed 160 search warrants on pot patches across Ontario; in 2001 that number jumped to 650.

Many of those warrants were for hydroponic pot-growing operations typically set up in the converted basements and garages of suburban rental homes. In Vancouver police estimate that there are as many as 3,000 of these clandestine greenhouses. Their main product is B.C. Bud, a generic, non-trademarked name for several strains of very potent pot. Long cultivated throughout B.C., it's now also showing up in the pot-growing regions of the Ottawa Valley and southeastern Quebec. The B.C. Bud industry is thriving: both American and Canadian law enforcement officials say that it's B.C.'s number-one farm industry, and the second-most important cash crop in Canada (after wheat). The business may also be the province's largest employer—but the people involved in it aren't in the habit of keeping records to share with the authorities or the media.

Seed growers and sellers are rarely bothered by the police, and advertise openly in pot specialty publications such as the Vancouver-based *Cannabis Culture*, which, incidentally, has been one of the more successful Canadian entrants into the U.S. magazine market.

As a cash crop, pot's attraction is its ability to deliver high profits at relatively low risk. The maximum penalty in Canada for growing pot is seven years, but most convicted growers spend only a few months in jail. Anyone charged with a lesser offence, such as owning a few plants for personal use, usually gets only house arrest or a suspended sentence. Even some grow-house operators have been able to talk their way into suspended sentences or terms of house arrest.

Those relatively low penalties make Canada a haven for American pot growers. But the U.S. Drug Enforcement Administration is fighting the Canadian pot industry: it has set up special enforcement zones in the Pacific Northwest, and is pressuring the Canadian government to share information and crack down on growers. Under pressure from the United States, Canadian police have joined the Integrated Border Enforcement Team (IBET), which comprises DEA officers, U.S. Customs Service and Border Patrol agents, and the RCMP. Armed with weapons, scopes, night goggles, and audio equipment (as are the smugglers), IBET patrols the highways between the ports of entry to intercept anyone engaging in the bud trade.

Because of this official scrutiny, getting B.C. Bud across the border doubles its value: from US $2,000 a pound in Vancouver to $4,000 in Portland, Oregon. If Canadian pot makes it to the major markets of Southern California, it's worth $6,000 to $7,000. In fact, it's in such demand in Los Angeles and San Diego that some dealers there are willing to travel to the U.S. Pacific Northwest and trade cocaine for it, pound for pound.

That way, the dealers reduce their risk from the law—getting caught in California with a pound of cocaine will net a much longer prison sentence than being busted with a pound of marijuana—while making the same money for dealing B.C. Bud out in fractions of ounces. (It's even more profitable when cut with cheap Mexican pot, which sells for one-tenth the price.)

But growers of B.C. Bud are facing increasing heat, and not all from police. Biker gangs and Asian street gangs are trying to control the business, and some growers have been badly hurt in home invasion robberies. Most members of Vancouver's large and busy dope-growing community, though, say that the police are being alarmist about pot producers. "Last year [2001], both the RCMP and the Canadian Association of Chiefs of Police endorsed decriminalization of marijuana possession," says Neil Boyd, a professor of criminology at Simon Fraser University. "But this year [2002], some police forces have taken to the media to demonize grow-ops. We're told that growers are members of organized crime syndicates who steal hydro, risk electrocuting themselves or others, deprive children of oxygen, invite home invasions, and start fires. Are there just some bad apples in this counter-culture industry—or do all growers threaten all neighborhoods?"

Boyd says that domestic growers have actually helped cut the role of international organized crime in marijuana production, importing, and distribution. "Thirty years ago, the Canadian marijuana industry was largely based on import-export transactions," he points out. "Hashish was shipped to Canada from Lebanon and Afghanistan, and marijuana from Jamaica, Colombia, Thailand, and California. That trade continues today; but domestic cultivation has taken over, supplying most of the domestic market and a small part of the international market."

Prohibition is profitable for the law enforcement industry, which has grown as more cops and prison guards have been hired to fight the War on Drugs. But it has also kept marijuana prices artificially high, thereby making the industry a magnet for criminals attracted to the big profits. "Drug dealers are not exactly the most socially responsible people—but is all this worth it?" he asks. "The War on Drugs costs hundreds of millions a year for enforcement, imprisonment, courtrooms and lawyers, not to mention the human costs of conviction and imprisonment. But the benefits? Nothing jumps to mind immediately."

Canada remains in the forefront of the hemp revival and in the marijuana decriminalization fight. The Canadian justice minister promised in 2002 that he would introduce a law to decriminalize possession of small amounts of marijuana, and drug testing in most workplaces has been outlawed. The Canadian Human Rights Commission ruled in 2002 that random and pre-employment drug testing of public employees is a human rights violation and not allowed under the Canadian *Human Rights Act*. Its decision struck down drug-testing policies for federally regulated workers, such as bank employees and airline pilots. Workers in the Canadian federal government and the people working in the industries it regulates became the first employees in North America to be protected from the arbitrary search of their bodies for traces of drugs.

"Positive drug tests simply confirm an individual's previous exposure to drugs, not whether the person is capable of performing the essential requirements of their job," the commission stated in a press release the day the decision was made public. "The Canadian *Human Rights Act* prohibits discrimination based upon disability or perceived disability, and drug and alcohol dependency are considered disabilities under the law."

It found policies that result in an employee's automatic loss of employment or reassignment, or that impose "inflexible reinstatement conditions without regard for personal circumstances" are also likely in violation of the law. Post-accident testing, workplace drug testing for "reasonable" cause, and random alcohol testing for safety-sensitive employees are generally still allowed, the commission ruled. Drug tests that are used to "weed out" and destroy the livelihoods of people who turn out to have a trace of a drug in their body are repellent to people who believe in individual liberty. Still, they're part of the U.S. government's War on Drugs.

There are ways around drug tests, some of them likely more effective than others. Pot culture magazines offer a variety of test-beaters. *High Times* offers a drug-test hotline at $1.95 per minute that advises callers on the latest testing procedures, the amount of time it takes for drug residues to leave the body, substances that can give false positives, and cleansing products that can rid blood and urine of drug residues. The magazine says more than 150,000 customers have used the service since 1996.

And there are test-foiling kits on the market; Urinetheclear tells fearful pot smokers: "Stop wasting your money on adulterants and detoxifiers. Labs now test for their presence. Instead, give them what they really want, genuine drug-free human urine, prepackaged in a concealable vinyl pouch with routing tube. Completely undetectable, even in observed testing situations."

The kit comes with a heating element and temperature strip that keeps the urine at body temperature for up to 10 hours. The urine is shipped frozen or dehydrated (user's choice), with enough for two tests. The company will ship the kit to all states except South Carolina (see below) and donates a dollar of the US $70 price to the World Trade Center Relief Fund. And, if the system fails, the company offers a 300 percent refund, which will cover the cost of a lot of résumés.

The company's best ad shows the Statue of Liberty holding a vial of the company's product. That image was dropped after September 11, 2001, when the company became a bit more respectful of monuments.

The Whizzinator, sold from Long Beach, California, offers synthetic urine, similarly kept warm and in place by a heated body pouch. The fake urine is supposed to be able to pass all laboratory tests. The sellers of the Urinator claim their device is the original drug-test beater. It can be worn every day, as long as the batteries that run the heating device for the synthetic urine are replaced regularly. The Urinovator goes even farther: it comes with a plastic penis that, according to its makers, looks so real that it can't be shown in a family head magazine. This little miracle of science and art costs $100. Its moving parts are reusable.

Clear Choice, in Alpharetta, Georgia, sells synthetic urine and a heat activator. Its makers remind customers that the sale of real human urine is banned in South Carolina, Texas, Nebraska, and Pennsylvania, but there's no law against selling the faux stuff. And, in another dig at the competition, Clear Choice warns that chemical reaction-fueled heating pads used by some kits to heat real urine to body temperature can burn tender skin in sensitive places and can ruin a sample by keeping it too hot or too cold. Instead, their product is in a small bottle with its own little heat activator that's kept stashed in a pocket.

For people who don't want to go to the trouble of stashing real or fake urine in their underwear, there are several lines of detoxification juices, drinks, shampoos, tablets, and health food supplements—but they're not cheap. Formula 1, rush-delivered from Health Tech in Alpharetta, Georgia, by the same people who make the Clear Choice fake urine kit, costs $35 a bottle, but there's a small discount for buying in bulk. The stuff is supposed to work in an hour to get marijuana residue out of blood and urine. It lasts for up to five hours and comes in "tasty pina colada or cran-apple cocktail flavor." There's extra strength for people "with higher toxin levels and/or larger body mass." And, if it fails to live up to the sales pitch, the company promises to give you twice your money back.

Urine Luck, made by Spectrum Labs in Cincinnati, Ohio, is a little vial of chemicals that is supposed to kill off any pot residues before the testee hands over the sample. The same company makes Quick Fizz one-hour detoxifying tablets, Absolute De-Tox Carbo Mix one-hour flush drink, home drug test kits, and Urine Luck "Pass Any Drug Test" T-shirts. Presumably, only the unwise wear these shirts to work or while crossing international borders.

Some other entrepreneurs offer drug test kits to let smokers know whether they'd pass a government or employer drug test. Most look like pregnancy tests, and within a few minutes can tell whether there's enough marijuana, cocaine, amphetamines, PCP, or opiates in the system to trigger a positive.

Farmers in Canada and Europe are currently reviving hemp strains, breeding new varieties, and developing the labor-saving technologies that will make hemp a competitive crop.

In June 1994, southern Ontario farmer Joe Stroebel and his partner Geof Kime, owner-operators of Hempline Inc., sowed five varieties of low-THC hemp from Europe under license from the Canadian Ministry of Health on six acres of sandy loam soil in a part of the province that was the country's largest tobacco producer. Their pioneering efforts inspired 12 other Canadian farmers to grow hemp in four provinces in 1995.

The federal government has revised 60-year-old laws to allow tightly controlled cultivation of hemp. Growers needed tough background checks and had to promise to protect their fields from thieves who might try stealing hemp flower tops. Farmers must even pay into a fund for extra police protection of growing areas. In order to launch the ground-breaking pilot project, Hempline Inc. cultivated support from private-citizen hemp-activist groups such as H.E.M.P. Canada and the Hemp Futures Study Group. Using data supplied by the hemp advocacy groups, prominent Canadian lawyer Allan Young helped to navigate Hempline through the bureaucratic maze, convincing public servants and politicians to give the company the first Canadian hemp licenses in three generations.

Canadian hemp growers are the only people on the North American continent who can legally grow hemp, but they must have a license to cultivate it, another one to distribute cannabis products such as oil and fiber, and a license to import hemp seed. To be profitable, Canadian hemp farms need to export their hemp across the border to the United States, where the raw hemp fibers and oil are tested to make sure they have no THC.

Police visit fields regularly to make spot checks and take samples that are tested for THC. Canadian hemp farmers find the crop does well in Canada's short, hot summers. The plants grow 2 or 3 inches (5 to 7.5 centimeters) a day, reaching about 12 feet (3 meters) in 75 days. The plants that are grown for fiber are cut before seeds form and produce 2.0 to 3.5 tons of dried stalk per acre, about the same as hemp yields in Europe and Asia. Further field trials may well lead to an increase in both fiber quality and yield. The first crop of Canadian hemp was made into wallboard in a factory in Oregon.

Within five years of Hempline's first crop, hemp farming had spread throughout Ontario, and the government began retreating from its earlier position that hemp was a potentially dangerous crop. Farmers who planted some 35,000 acres of hemp in 2002 were among the few cash crop growers who made a decent return on their investment. Commodity prices for traditional crops were at their lowest levels in generations. Canadian hemp growers quickly seized on the lack of competition from farmers in the U.S. and started local food and fiber industries. Canadian farmers have mixed feelings about the U.S. hemp ban. They realize they've been given a rare opportunity to supply the bulk of the raw material for the annual $200 million U.S. hemp product trade, but they also know that many honest would-be hemp farmers in the U.S. are being kept from planting. As well, the shortage of hemp and the continued stubbornness of U.S. authorities slows research into hemp product development.

Hemp farms now operate on the Canadian prairies. So far, there's been only one glitch: in 1995, an unlicensed hemp farm in British Columbia was raided and the crop seized. However, in the years since Canada began allowing the legal cultivation of hemp, there has not been a single case reported of crop theft, illicit marijuana growing, or any of the other problems that anti-hemp authorities say are linked with hemp farming.

How long can Canada remain a haven for Americans who are fed up with the U.S. government's 65-year-old battle with the cannabis plant? The national and powerful provincial governments are under tough pressure from the U.S. administration to toe the American line. Both the Clinton and the Bush administrations warned Canada to toughen its enforcement of anti-marijuana laws and bust grow houses. The Canadian government has made it clear that it wants to end the practice of tagging pot smokers with criminal records. Instead, it would follow the British practice of levying a fine through a system similar to traffic enforcement. The American response has been to threaten to tighten border security and strangle trade between Canada and its much more powerful neighbor.

U.S. Drug Czar Barry McCaffrey insists, in his pleadings with Canadian officials, that marijuana is dangerous because it's addictive. That claim is debatable, but even if it's true, THC joins a list that includes nicotine, alcohol, caffeine, and many prescription drugs. "There's not a question about whether marijuana is a dependency-producing substance today," John Walters, the previous Drug Czar said while on a visit to Canada in 2002 to try to talk the government into backing off from its decriminalization policy. "Some people seem to be living with the view of the reefer-madness '70s." It was another verbal volley over the border in an escalating debate on effective drug strategies. Walters said border security in the United States is being heightened to stop the flow of drugs and terrorism. "The issue for us is that Canada has become a major supplier of certain drugs," he said. "We're worried about the common health of our citizens. But we're, in the United States, mostly worried about obviously our own citizens, as we should be. We have major supply coming in from Canada that's growing and we need to get on top of it." Deputy Prime Minister John Manley, who is in charge of U.S.–Canada border relations, said he is not aware of a specific threat from the United States to tighten the border in response to the proposed relaxation of marijuana laws. Manley, though, shuttled to Washington in 2003 to meet with U.S. Homeland Security Director Tom Ridge and DEA officials to try to keep Canada from becoming a scapegoat in both the "War on Terror" and the "War on Drugs."

DECRIMINALIZATION AND REACTION

Most American hemp advocates don't want to leave the country. They'd rather see some logic brought to the issue, but reintroducing hemp into the fields of the U.S. is a challenge that may be a long way off. Politically, hemp advocates must overcome the entrenched attitudes of the Drug Enforcement Administration, local police, industrial lobbies, powerful prison guard unions, fundamentalists, and others with a vested interest in maintaining a ban on cannabis. Opening the door to hemp cultivation and exploitation may (and probably should) deflate many of the myths about marijuana and the effectiveness of any sweeping prohibition.

Rather than deal with drug issues as health and social problems, current policies in most Western countries have made them moral issues. Governments have criminalized recreational users and addicts, treating them as offenders against society, applying the same stigmas and punishment used on thieves and wife-beaters. And, in many places, the sentences for drug possession are much more extreme than those imposed on people convicted of harming children. However, many politicians have gone so far down the road of fear mongering that there's no chance for them to save face. The War on Drugs has become a war on the poor, inner-city kids, people who wear hemp clothes, and people who grow a few pot plants and smoke pot in the privacy of their homes. It's created jobs for narcotics agents, prosecutors, jail guards, customs agents, narcotic snitches, and politicians. At the same time, this war has been an utter failure. It's no more difficult today to buy a chunk of hashish than it was 30 years ago, but the Drug Enforcement Administration continues to harass even the makers of hemp oil–based lip balms.

Even if hemp cultivation in the United States was re-legalized reviving the industry may be difficult. U.S. farmers have lost the germ plasm, the know-how, and the machinery for raising the crop. But, at the same time, it seems fair to expect the crop will find niches heretofore untapped, since environmental impact as a factor in consumer choice is a relatively new phenomenon.

Even with the ban on hemp cultivation and many legal restrictions on the use of the plant, U.S. domestic sales of imported hemp products take in an estimated $50 million a year. Farmers, hard-pressed by low crop prices and high overhead, see the potential: the American Farm Bureau Federation recently called hemp "one of the most promising crops in half a century." The movement to end prohibition is gathering support among voters and their representatives throughout the developed world. Hawaii has not only passed legislation allowing for hemp trials but has also planted the first legal hemp crop since the 1950s. The DEA's position is being opposed by some states, including Missouri, which, in 1996, passed its own *Hemp Production Act*, which would have established a hemp growing system similar to Canada's. In Wisconsin, the state's Agribusiness Council believes one million acres could be available for growing hemp in a crop rotation plan. However, Wisconsin won't be growing hemp until the federal government lifts its ban on hemp growing.

Although industrial hemp is currently legal in more than 25 countries just after the September 11, 2001, terrorist attacks on the United States, the Drug Enforcement Administration used its regulatory power to go after the industrial hemp industry. Critics of U.S. policy said the DEA chose that time because the public was fixated on the attacks and the attack on Afghanistan that followed soon afterward. The DEA ordered a ban on imports of all hemp products that could put any THC into the human body. Opponents of the DEA's actions fought to prevent the widening of the agency's hemp products ban, but the protest wasn't able to generate much publicity during that time of crisis. A Canadian company, Kenex Ltd., of Chatham, Ontario, filed a $20 million claim under the North America Free Trade Agreement's Chapter 11, the section of the treaty that requires a "level playing field" for companies operating in Canada, the United States, and Mexico.

"The notice is a way of saying that we have a problem, and we want a solution. Once it was filed, the sides involved have three months to work it out," Todd Weiler, a Toronto-based lawyer representing Kenex, said. "Our (NAFTA) Chapter 11 claim says that it's unfair the way the Drug Enforcement Administration has gone about banning these products, that what they did was not fair and equitable. Under NAFTA, foreigners have to be given the same treatment as citizens of a signatory country. People in the U.S. can sell poppy seeds, which contain very minute traces of opium, a controlled substance, while my clients can't sell hemp seeds, which contain minute traces of THC [the psychoactive ingredient in marijuana]. That's not fair.

"Originally, the DEA proposed a rule that any product that had hemp in it was gone. Now, they say anything that has hemp in it can stay, as long as you can prove it doesn't enter the body. They believe all hemp and marijuana is the same thing. The truth is the opposite. And they claim that hemp products give false positives for THC on drug tests. That's not true at all."

Canada requires hemp products to be labeled. Stems, seeds, or flowers of industrial hemp plants can contain no more than 0.3 percent THC. Marijuana contains between 10 and 30 per cent THC. Kenex also argues that it's being penalized because it won't be able to ship its hemp seed oil across the border, even though the oil can still be used in soap and cosmetics that do not put THC into the body, even if there is a trace in the oil. Although hemp growing is banned in the U.S., the industry is worth more than $50 million a year in that country.

The Canadian government has supported its hemp producers. Canadian trade officials recently warned the DEA that its ban is an attack on a legal, regulated Canadian industry. Canada says the DEA rules violate World Trade Organization requirements that countries conduct risk-assessment tests before prohibiting products. Canada has allowed commercial farming of hemp since 1998 and has actively encouraged farmers, many of them ex-tobacco growers, to plant it.

The DEA's hemp prohibition is also being fought by the U.S. hemp-food industry. It's a $5-million-a-year business, which was rapidly growing until the ban. Stores in the United States were just starting to sell novelty and organic foods such as Hemp Chips, Hempmylk, Healthy Hemp Sprouted Bread, Hemp Plus Granola Bars, and Hempzel Pretzels.

In America, actor/activist Woody Harrelson is one anti-prohibition protester who has raised the visibility of the hemp movement. In 2001 a jury in the small Kentucky town of Beattyville threw out marijuana cultivation charges against Harrelson, despite a ruling by Kentucky's highest court that the state's law prohibiting marijuana cultivation also bans the cultivation of hemp. The six-member jury took only 20 minutes to find Harrelson not guilty of a misdemeanor charge of possession of marijuana.

"That wasn't marijuana he planted, if he planted anything," juror Sylvia Caldwell (no known relation to Samuel) said as she left Lee District Court with Harrelson's autograph on a piece of hemp paper. The 39-year-old actor showed up for his trial in a dark hemp suit. The case began on June 1, 1996, when Harrelson wielded a grubbing hoe to challenge the law, which does not distinguish between marijuana and hemp. Harrelson won in lower courts, but the state's high court overturned the ruling. Harrelson faced up to a year in jail and a $500 fine for his protest. Former Kentucky governor Louie Nunn, one of Harrelson's four attorneys, challenged the law in his closing argument when he held up a candy bar made from hemp seeds, then took a small bite. "Now I've got it in me and I've got it on me," he said to the jury. "If you think Mr. Harrelson should be put in jail for one year or one week or even one night, I guess we'll be there together."

Lee County Attorney Tom Jones said a videotape of Harrelson holding out the seeds before planting them, and his repeated statements that he was challenging the law, proved he knew he was committing a crime. He asked the jury to convict the actor and give him the maximum fine and at least 30 days in jail. "Mr. Harrelson has this coming," Jones said. "He misused his fame." Later, Jones said he likes Harrelson, but the actor was "guilty as sin." Jones said Harrelson had another motive: using legalized hemp as a stepping stone to legalized marijuana. Harrelson agreed that he supports legalizing marijuana, but said, "it's a totally separate issue."

Nunn, who had never seen Harrelson's acting work before he started to work on the case, said he took the case for free because he supports hemp as a crop for Kentucky farmers. He told jurors that the authors of the Constitution set up the jury system as a safeguard against bad laws or biased judges. "What's important here today is to see the blessings of liberty guaranteed in the Constitution are carried out," he said. "What you do here today will go out all over this nation. It will say whether justice will prevail." His hemp battle in Kentucky is over, Harrelson said.

He turned the fight over to Nunn, who said that some legislators who support hemp have "political apprehensions" about voting for it. Charles Beal II, another of Harrelson's attorneys, suggested the law might still be changed to allow hemp cultivation in Kentucky. "When the law changes, Woody would be the first to come back and plant it legally," he said.

Hemp growers have at least one designer-label buyer. Italian designer Giorgio Armani has given money to a consortium of farmers, seed producers, and industrialists to restart hemp cultivation in the Italian countryside. Armani has already started using hemp imported from France for his collections.

The Italian project started in 2002 with the sowing of 500 acres near the city of Ferrara, Italy. Armani's group will build a factory for processing the hemp. That factory will have the capacity to handle the produce from 2500 acres. The Italian government says it won't license any more than 2500 acres for hemp growing so, if Armani needs more fabric, he'll have to get it from farmers in Europe or Canada, who already have no trouble selling their crops.

Despite the hemp revival in the rest of the developed world, the United States and some state governments continue to fight hemp growing. Sometimes they go to absurd lengths to silence proponents of the plant, such as Harrelson.

Shelby County school officials fired a teacher who twice had Harrelson talk to her fifth-grade class about industrial hemp. For five years, the state of Kentucky and school teacher Donna Cockrel were locked in a court fight similar to the 1920s Scopes Monkey Trial in neighboring Tennessee. Cockrel was fired in 1997 for letting Harrelson come into her class and talk about hemp growing. Shelby is part of a region in Kentucky where hemp was grown for more than a century, until the crop was legislated from the fields. She found a new job teaching in Detroit, but is fighting to prove that her firing violates her First Amendment right to freedom of speech. In fall 2002, the United

States Supreme Court stopped the state's appeals and ordered the lawsuit to go ahead.

The school board also accused Cockrel of insubordination, conduct unbecoming a teacher, and neglect of duty. The school district alleged she called her principal profane names in front of others, that she denied remedial services to some students, and denigrated students in front of others. Authorities also tried to have her thrown out of the teaching profession. She sued the school system in 1998, arguing that her firing violated her constitutional right of free speech and was a breach of her contract as a tenured teacher. She contended she was let go simply because of "her classroom and public statements about industrial hemp."

Cockrel invited Harrelson to give students a lesson on alternative crops that could help save the environment. He visited the school several times in 1996 and 1997. Harrelson's visits drew heavy media coverage and intense criticism in the community. Parents removed students from the school during the second visit, and the school's PTA called for Cockrel's dismissal. In May 1999, Kentucky's Education Professional Standards Board, which polices teachers, suspended Cockrel's teaching certificate, retroactive to 1997 when she was fired. In July 2001, the standards board reversed itself and reinstated her certificate. The wrongful-dismissal lawsuit is still grinding through the courts.

Meanwhile, bureaucrats continue to pester hemp entrepreneurs, such as John Roulac, a Sebastopol, California, businessman. Roulac owns and operates a company that imports industrial-grade hemp seeds and hemp oil. In February 2002, he was trying to bring a shipment of hemp seeds south across the Canadian border. His plan was to mix the sterilized seeds in chips and candy bars that his company, Nutiva Inc., sells to the health food supermarket chains Whole Foods and Wild Oats, among others.

But it just wasn't that easy, as Roulac found out when he became an unwilling combatant in the drug war. The seeds were legal to import. They were grown by Kenex, which has a spotless history in Canada as a hemp entrepreneur and seed producer. The company is one of the largest hemp exporters to the United States, and even though it is challenging the DEA over its proposed ban of edible hemp products, the company has been a good corporate citizen.

"I had to make something like 50 phone calls over three days," recalls Roulac, who finally convinced U.S. customs officials that the seeds, which contain faint trace amounts of THC, couldn't possibly get anyone high and are a legal product. Roulac says that the government's aggressive, "zero-tolerance" anti-drug policies are stifling legitimate trade that has nothing to do with the multibillion commerce in illicit drugs. "It's a constant minefield," he said. "The government throws up roadblocks to this business. They hassle us at the border. When you're a small company, you need to move your product fast." He says it's hard to find investors and customers when there's a constant danger that he'll be bankrupted by a new rule or an expensive court case. "If there's a chance that a product is illegal, many businesses, even pro-hemp health food stores, don't want it."

In New York, hemp activists had to go to court in 2002 to prove they couldn't get stoned on hemp seed pretzels and candy bars that they ate and gave away during a pro-hemp demonstration in front of a police station. Judge Langston McKinney threw out the charges against Jennifer Copeland, Patrick Head, and Gerrit Cain after experts testified that the miniscule amount of THC in the food could not affect the brain. Marijuana possession charges were lodged after a sheriff's deputy tested one of the candy bars, which showed positive for the presence of marijuana. Subsequent lab tests, however, were negative, and under New York State standards the presence of THC must be found for a case to proceed.

If hemp cultivation were legalized, could it really save U.S. farms and change the way we get food oils, proteins, and fiber? It's unclear, but legislators in more than 20 states have asked for research. They know that a year after Canada allowed hemp cultivation in 1998, production had doubled; it has redoubled every year since with no drop in price. The U.S. has taken a different approach to the plant, one that reflects the quick, unproven, and often unrealistic assumptions of the War on Drugs.

In mid-2001, a *USA Today*/CNN/Gallup poll showed 34 percent of Americans favored legalizing marijuana use, while 62 percent were opposed. It was the highest level of support for legalization since pollsters began asking the question in 1969. Support for legalization had been constant at about 25 percent for 20 years and moved up to 31 percent in August 2000. Activists said the debate on medical marijuana had focused public attention on the question of whether marijuana is dangerous.

Since 1996, voters in eight states have passed initiatives supporting medical marijuana. Polls show more than 70 percent of voters support medical marijuana. The poll found support for legalization highest among 18- to 49-year-olds, people in the West, and independent voters.

But not all conservatives oppose the government's failed prohibition program. Texas Republican congressman Ron Paul, a medical doctor with strong Libertarian beliefs, said last year:

Throughout our early history, a policy of minding our own business and avoiding entangling alliances, as George Washington admonished, was more representative of American ideals than those we have pursued for the past 50 years. Some sincere Americans have suggested that our modern interventionist policy set the stage for the attacks of 9–11, and for this, they are condemned as being unpatriotic. Another reason the hearts of many Americans are heavy with grief is because they dread what might come from the many new and broad powers the Government is demanding in the name of providing security. Daniel Webster once warned, "Human beings will generally exercise power when they can get it, and they will exercise it most undoubtedly in popular governments under pretence of public safety."

In the last 30 years, we have spent hundreds of billions of dollars on a failed war on drugs. This war has been used as an excuse to attack our liberties and privacy. It has been an excuse to undermine our financial privacy while promoting illegal searches and seizures with many innocent people losing their lives and property. Seizure and forfeiture have harmed a great number of innocent American citizens. Another result of this unwise war has been the corruption of many law enforcement officials. It is well known that with the profit incentives so high, we are not even able to keep drugs out of our armed prisons. Making our whole society a prison would not bring success to this floundering war on drugs. Sinister motives of the profiteers and gangsters, along with prevailing public ignorance, keeps this futile war going.

Illegal and artificially high priced drugs drive the underworld to produce, sell and profit from this social depravity. Failure to recognize that drug addiction, like alcoholism, is a disease rather than a crime, encourages the drug warriors in efforts that have not and will not ever work. We learned the hard way about alcohol prohibition and crime, but we have not yet seriously considered it in the ongoing drug war. Corruption associated with the drug dealers is endless. It has involved our police, the military, border guards and the judicial system. It has affected government policy and our own CIA. The artificially high profits from illegal drugs provide easy access to funds for rogue groups involved in fighting civil wars throughout the world.

Paul said that, for the first 140 years of U.S. history, the country had essentially no federal war on drugs, and far fewer problems with drug addiction and related crimes "as a consequence. In the past 30 years, even with the hundreds of billions of dollars spent on the drug war, little good has come of it. We have vacillated from efforts to stop the drugs at the source to severely punishing the users, yet nothing has improved. This war has been behind most big government policies of the last 30 years, with continual undermining of our civil liberties and personal privacy." Those who support the IRS's efforts to collect maximum revenues and root out the underground economy have welcomed this intrusion, even as the drug underworld grows in size and influence. Paul continued:

The drug war encourages violence. Government violence against non-violent users is notorious and has led to the unnecessary prison overpopulation. Innocent taxpayers are forced to pay for all this so-called justice. Our eradication project through spraying around the world, from Colombia to Afghanistan, breeds resentment because normal crops and good land can be severely damaged. Local populations perceive that the efforts and the profiteering remain somehow beneficial to our own agenda in these various countries.

CHAPTER 4

Growing Your Own

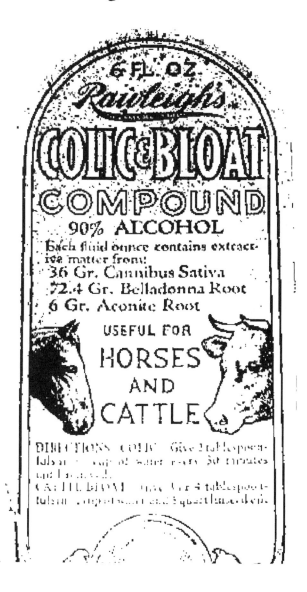

People who live in areas where marijuana possession is not a criminal offence or who have a prescription for medicinal cannabis may want to grow their own. People who choose to grow their own marijuana in areas where it's still illegal may face some form of criminal sanction if caught, but the upside is the control that growers have over the quality and purity of their marijuana. Growing pot in highly populated areas and places where police are very active can be stressful to the point of unpleasantness. However, with a bit of planning and some simple common sense, maintaining a small patch can be a fun and rewarding summer pastime.

Both the male and the female plant produce THC resin, although the resin made by the male is not as strong as that generated by the female. In a good crop, the male will still be potent enough to smoke. Marijuana can reach a height of 20 feet (6 m) and reach 4½ inches (11.5 m) in diameter. You do not want to grow plants this big. The ideal plant for the home gardener is fairly short, bushy, with plenty of flowering buds. The male plant dies in the 12th week of growing. The female will live another three to five weeks to generate seeds and can weigh twice as much as mature males.

OUTDOOR GROWING

Marijuana is a "photo-period" determinate plant. The plant has the natural ability to tell when the days are lengthening and shortening. Ideally, they will flower when there are twelve hours of uninterrupted darkness. In mid-latitudes, that flowering time falls around the end of September and into early October. Unfortunately, in higher altitudes of the United States and in many parts of Canada, that's also the time when the first hard frosts are a real possibility. However, there are "earlier" varieties that flower at ten hours of darkness and still produce high-potency buds.

A simple hydroponics system can be made in a single pot.

When you pick out a strain, you'll also want to shop for types of marijuana that are not susceptible to mold. Indica-dominant plants tend to be most likely to be ruined by mold, while sativa-dominant are slower to mature. Several seed companies will ship seeds and give advice. Since they are always under legal pressures, these seed sellers tend to change addresses. You will probably be able to find their temporary Internet addresses through a web search. Be sure that your seeds do not cross international borders or otherwise attract the professional interests of narcotics agents.

While marijuana plants are hardy, they're best started indoors. It's at this stage of the growing cycle that most people murder their plants, usually by over-watering them. Use one fluorescent every two trays of seedlings or clones (cuttings). Use well-drained soil in peat moss pots and plant one or two seeds in each one so you can transport the seedlings individually. Each seed should be planted about a half inch from the surface of the soil.

When you're looking for a place to put your plants, two factors are pivotal: security and sunlight. You probably do not want your plants to be found by authorities or by interlopers. And, without sunlight, the plants won't grow well. You'll need to look for a south-facing slope away from bike paths, hiking trails, areas where people pick berries or gather mushrooms, and places where kids like to play. You may want to take the risk of planting them among your tomatoes or raspberries, but, if you do, make sure you have just a few plants. That way, if you do become embroiled in a legal hassle, you can argue convincingly that the plants are for your own use. Most serious growers put their plants on other people's land or, if they live on farms, transplant their seedlings to a remote corner, so if the plants are found, they can plead ignorance of them.

If you're going to follow the "Johnny Potseed" route and sow your plants away from your home, spread them around. You may want to plant them near water, but far enough back from a lake or stream to be away from damp soil, animals, fisher-folks, and kids. Wherever you put your plants, make sure you don't literally beat a path to the spot. These can be seen from the air.

Pot growers very quickly develop a rather negative view of their fellow citizens, who, in the minds of many marijuana horti-culturalists, can be lumped into one of two groups: those "good citizens" who will eagerly report their patch to the police, and the no-so-good citizens who will steal their plants.

Marijuana plants need plenty of sunlight to thrive.

When you do settle on candidate spots, you must check the soil. Does it drain well? Marijuana is very susceptible to root rot. Does it get light through the entire day? A small clearing may get some light while you're there, but will your plants be in darkness a few hours later? Are you planting in a low-lying area that may be hit by an early frost? You may want to plant on the slope of a valley, but stay away from the bottom, where cold air collects. If you find the perfect spot but the soil isn't up to snuff, work on it in the fall and use it the following spring. If you are very ambitious, you may want to remove the topsoil, take out the subsoil and replace it with better-quality dirt. That way, the marijuana taproot will grow into soil that's rich in nutrients. You may, however, decide to make up in volume what you lose by lack of labor.

Still, even if you're not prepared to make major changes to the soil, you may want to take soil samples to nurseries to check for pH and nitrogen levels. You'll probably end up enriching the soil with perlite and vermiculite (but be careful, since these stand out in wild areas. Make sure they're covered with a layer of dirt), dolomite or hydrated lime (to lower pH), blood meal, compost, or worm castings to increase fertility. Leave a slight depression around the plants to catch and hold water.

If you have a mother plant, you may decide to take cuttings, or clones, from it. Some growers believe these plants are not as hardy, but with the huge variety of marijuana strains on the market, cloning gives you control over what type of plant you're growing. Growing plants from cuttings takes practice, but kits are available at most nurseries. Plant your seedlings when they are between 10 to 14 inches (25 to 35 cm) tall, or about six inches (15 cm) if they are rooted cuttings.

Most problems with plants are caused by overenthusiasm: overwatering of seedlings; putting plants out too early and losing them to frost; overuse of fertilizers; making too many visits to the patch. Plants that are transplanted late will be smaller than those that are planted just after the threat of frost passes, but the late transplants will mature earlier. Most people get the timing right through trial and error.

Use a mixture of water and plant food up till the day you plant your seedlings or clones. Then, leave the patch alone for at least a week. On your next visit, feed the plants with 20-20-20 fertilizer and a Vitamin B1 supplement. Watch the weather. If it's a dry summer, you'll need to go back and water the plants, a task that's best done in the evening. You may also want to add a bit of 20-20-20 plant food once a week during that first month, as this is a time when the plant is doing most of its growing. Once the plant flowers, switch from 20-20-20 to Vita-Max.

You may run into trouble with pests. Diatomacious earth is a good, natural way to get rid of most insects and slugs. The sharp edges of the fossil diatoms, a form of plankton, cut into the shells of insects. It's sold as a white powder. Old copper wiring placed around the base of the plants will deter slugs.

Most herbivores will take a professional interest in your plants, and there's very little you can do to stop them. Some growers use human urine (usually their own) to keep larger animals away. One grower suggests bringing a bottle of pee with you so you can make a 20-foot (6-m)-diameter circle around the plants. Human hair also carries scents that frighten off some animals, as does soap and perfume. Don't, however, leave so much hair and cosmetics around your patch that it stands out. Some serious growers buy fox or coyote urine from hunting supply stores to scare off mice, rabbits, gophers, and other small animals. How the sellers obtain this urine is a mystery to me, but it's probably much easier to buy it than to collect it yourself.

Molds and fungus are big trouble. Mold will kill your plant within days. If you find mold, harvest your plant immediately, salvage what you can of the bud, but make sure you have stripped away all mold.

Serious growers like to grow a small variety of strains that finish throughout the season, harvesting buds from the time the first ones form until the last of the late varieties are threatened by frost. Then, after harvesting your buds, hang them in an attic to dry or place them in a brown paper bag and leave the bag in a dry place for a few days. The brown bag works for any kind of herb.

Most people who garden get a great feeling of satisfaction from watching their plants grow. With common sense, growing your own pot should be a rewarding experience. Don't let failure get you down or let carelessness cause you legal problems.

INDOOR GROWING

When the Canadian government decided to grow medical marijuana, it chose the indoor route. In fact, the locale was very indoors, at the bottom of a mine in the sub-arctic community of Flin Flon, Manitoba. If nothing else, the experiment proved you can grow marijuana everywhere.

You do not need to move to Flin Flon, Manitoba, to be a successful indoor grower. In fact, the very quiet house down the block may well be the indoor farm of very successful entrepreneurial pot growers. Growing indoors—especially small amounts that don't send power use soaring—gives cultivators some peace of mind. The crop is less likely to be found, insects and animals are not likely to be a problem, and you don't have to fight the temptation to visit your plants several times a day.

Some growers choose to grow their pot in pots, but hydroponics is much more effective. Hydroponics is the name given to the various techniques for growing plants without soil. Since, as one wag said, the British will cultivate the ash heaps of Hades if the devil lets them, it's not surprising that hydroponics is a growing method pioneered by bored British sailors stuck on isolated islands. The sailors realized plants take in their nutrients as simple inorganic ions, and that soil, while a source for such nutrients, was not essential. All nutrients that enter a plant through the roots must be already dissolved in the plant's water supply. Botanists have developed various mixtures of chemicals that are mixed with water and brought to plants through feeder systems. With the right nutrients and light levels, any kind of herb can thrive in a home garden.

Some types of hydroponic systems use relatively inert material as a physical support for the plant roots. Other techniques dispense altogether with any growing medium, delivering nutrient solution directly to the roots, by a variety of methods.

In a passive hydroponics system, the simplest form, the

plant is grown in a container of growing medium. The container stands in a tray of nutrient solution, which is absorbed through holes in the container. The medium generally has large air spaces, allowing ample oxygen to the roots, and capillary action delivers water and nutrients to the roots. A variety of materials can be used for the medium: vermiculite, perlite, clay granules, rockwool (which is used in aquarium filters), and gravel. Newer media on the market are coir fiber and cocoa bean shells.

This is not a labor-intensive way to grow plants. Once it's set up, it needs some topping up and the occasional replacement of the nutrient solution. Kits are available from most nurseries and from shops that cater to pot growers. As well, they're sold on the Internet.

Raft cultivation involves growing plants on sheets of expanded polystyrene with holes drilled through them. Young plants are placed in the holes with the roots hanging down. The sheet then floats in a shallow tank of nutrient solution. The tank is kept aerated by an air pump to ensure the roots have adequate oxygen.

With the Nutrient Film Technique, the plants grow through light-proof plastic films placed over shallow, gently sloping channels. A steady flow of nutrients is maintained along the channel, and the roots grow into dense mats, with a thin film of nutrient passing over them (hence the name of the technique).

More serious growers will likely choose the Flood and Drain (or Ebb and Flow) hydroponics system. In its simplest form, there is a tray above a reservoir of nutrient solution. The tray is either filled with growing medium (clay granules being the most common) and planted directly, or pots of medium stand in the tray. A timer triggers a pump to fill the upper tray with nutrients. After the plants feed, the nutrient mixture drains back down into the reservoir. This system keeps the medium regularly flushed with nutrients and air. Drip-feeding systems are similar to the flood-and-drain method, but the pump delivers a continuous trickle of nutrient onto the medium.

No matter which type of growing method you choose, be discreet. No matter how spectacular your crop, there are few fall fairs with "best bud" categories. However, there *are* some. Check magazines like *Cannabis Culture* and *High Times* for the one nearest you.

The World of Hemp

AUSTRALIA allows research crops. And in the state of Victoria, commercial production is now licensed.

AUSTRIA has a hemp industry, including production of hempseed oil and medicines.

CANADA started to license research crops in 1994 on an experimental basis. In addition to crops for fiber, one seed crop was experimentally licensed in 1995. Many acres were planted in 1997. Canada now licenses for commercial agriculture with over 35,000 acres (14,200 hectares) planted in 2002. The Canadian government plans to decriminalize possession of small amounts of marijuana, courts have ruled that prosecuting people for possession of marijuana for personal use is unconstitutional, and most workplace drug testing is illegal.

CHILE grows hemp mostly for seed oil production.

CHINA is the world's largest exporter of hemp paper and textiles.

DENMARK planted its first modern hemp trials in 1997. The country is committed to utilizing organic agriculture methods.

FINLAND has had a resurgence of hemp beginning in 1995 with several small test crops.

FRANCE harvested 10,000 tons in 1994. France is the main source of viable low-THC hempseed.

GERMANY banned hemp in 1982, but research on new hemp use began in 1992. The ban was lifted in 1995, and many technologies and products are being developed. Clothes and paper are currently made from imported raw materials. The German word for hemp is *hanf*.

GREAT BRITAIN lifted its hemp prohibition in 1993. Animal bedding, paper, and textiles have been developed. A government grant was given to develop new markets for natural fibers. Four thousand acres were grown in 1994. Subsidies of £230 per acre (£93 per hectare) are given by the government for growing. Possession of small amounts of marijuana carries a noncriminal fine penalty that is rarely imposed.

HUNGARY is rebuilding its 1,000-year-old hemp industry and is one of the biggest exporters of hemp cordage, rugs, and hemp fabric to the United States. Hungary also exports hemp seed and hemp paper.

INDIA has large stands of wild cannabis and uses it for cordage, textiles, and seed oil.

ITALY has, on a pilot project, licensed 2,500 acres (1,018 hectares) for hemp fiber cultivation. The crop will be made into cloth for, among others, designer Georgio Armani.

JAPAN has a religious tradition that requires that the Emperor wear hemp garments, so there is a small plot maintained for the imperial family only. Some hemp is legally grown in the central part of the country, but Japan continues to import hemp for cloth and artistic applications.

THE NETHERLANDS is conducting a four-year study to evaluate and test hemp for paper, and is developing processing equipment. Seed breeders are developing new strains of low-THC varieties. The Netherlands also has limited de facto decriminalization.

POLAND currently grows hemp for fabric and cordage and manufactures hemp particleboard. Farmers there, who have a long tradition of growing hemp, have demonstrated the benefits of using hemp to cleanse soils contaminated by heavy metals. Many of those toxic sites were left by the Russian army during its 45-year occupation.

ROMANIA is the largest commercial producer of hemp in Europe. Total cultivation area in 1993 was 40,000 acres (16,200 hectares). Some of it is exported to Hungary for processing. Romania also exports to Western Europe and the United States.

RUSSIA maintains the largest hemp germ plasm collection in the world at the N.I. Vavilov Scientific Research Institute of Plant Industry (VIR) in Saint Petersburg. The institute needs money to pay curators to maintain this collection and to prevent it from being lost.

SLOVENIA grows hemp and manufactures currency paper.

SPAIN grows and exports hemp pulp for paper and produces rope and textiles.

SWITZERLAND is one of Europe's major hemp producers.

EGYPT, KOREA, PORTUGAL, THAILAND, and UKRAINE also produce hemp.

UNITED STATES granted the first hemp permit in 40 years to Hawaii for an experimental quarter-acre (0.10 hectare) plot in 1999. Importers and manufacturers have thrived using imported raw materials. Legislatures in Vermont, Hawaii. North Dakota, Montana, Maine, Illinois. Virginia, California, Arizona, and Maryland have passed bills to support research into hemp cultivation. Three states — Colorado, Arkansas, and Missouri — have initiatives pending. As well, California and several other states have passed referendums supporting medical marijuana, but so far, the Supreme Court and the federal government have prevented these initiatives from being implemented.

Web Sites

Hempola
www.hempola.com
Hempola provides a wide range of hemp-based food and body-care products.

Living Tree Paper Company
www.livingtreepaper.com
Manufacturer of printing and stationery papers including Vanguard Recycled Plus, Vanguard Eco Blend, and Vanguard Hemp, which contain industrial hemp fiber.

Dr. Bronner's Magic Soaps
www.drbronner.com
Dr. Bronner's official web site. The liquid and bar soaps now contain hemp oil. Download Adobe Acrobat files of their product labels to read The Moral ABC.

Hempstores.com
www.hempstores.com
Search engine of hemp product retailers in North America. Search by state or province to find a store near you that carries hemp products.

Tribal Fiber
www.tribalfiber.com
Tribal Fiber is an ethical manufacturer of distinctive, handmade, naturally dyed hemp home accessories. Online retail sales.

The Ohio Hempery
www.hempery.com
Hemp clothes, fabric, paper, nutritional oil, and skin-care products. Online ordering.

The Natural Zone
www.the-naturalzone.com
Carries a variety of hemp pet products, paper products, body care, and accessories. Online retail sales and mail order.

Ecosource Paper Inc.
www.islandnet.com/~ecodette/ecosource.htm
Inkjet Laser Printing Cover Paper. Made from 40 percent hemp, 40 percent flax, 20 percent cotton linters in natural (oxygen bleached), white, and colors. High-quality printing, art, stationery, and gift wrap.

Hemp U.S. Flag
www.hempusflag.com
Supports VoteHemp.com voter education effort and promotes industrial hemp for environmental and social responsibility.

Hemp Supply Inc.
www.hempsupply.com
Bags, accessories, clothing, body care, twine, crafts, fabric, hemp information, and special offers.

MotherHemp Ltd
www.motherhemp.com
One of the largest providers of hemp-based products to the European market. Hemp oil, hemp seed, textiles, clothes, and many other industrial hemp products.

Galaxy Global Hempery
www.galaxyglobaleatery.com
The store has a variety of hemp foods and seeds, hemp oil–based soaps, shampoos, and skin products.

Hungry Bear Hemp Foods
www.efn.org/~eathemp
Hemp seed treats made in Oregon from imported and sterilized seeds.

Hemp Oil Canada
www.hempoilcan.com
Dedicated to the procurement, processing, marketing, and distribution of bulk hemp food products including hemp seed oil, hulled hemp seed, roasted and sterilized hemp seed, and seed cake products to local, national, and international markets.

Alterna Applied Research Labs
www.4alterna.com
Manufacturer's premium, professional salon-only hair-care products. Uses advanced ingredient technologies, enzyme therapy, nutrient-rich hemp seed oil, caviar extract for beautiful, healthy-looking hair.

Sunhemp
www.sunhemp.com
Hemp products ranging from clothing, twine, jewelry, bags, and bath and beauty products. Carries Nutiva shelled hemp seed and snack bars.

Smith Center
www.smithcenter.com
Manufactures balanced natural outerwear from fabrics such as hemp, hemp/cotton, organic cotton, 100 percent wool, and recycled fill.

Indian Hemp Jewelry and Accessories
www.indianhemp.net
Original designs. Wholesale and retail. Since 1975.

Hempooch Hemp for Pets
www.hempooch.com
Hemp pet accessories. Products include hemp collars, leashes, and toys for dogs and cats. Also offers tie-dye shirts for dogs and gift certificates.

Way Out Wax Candles
www.wayoutwax.com
Hemp, kaleidoscope, jar, aromatherapy, and beeswax candles and candle-making supplies. Online sales.

Mother Earth Enterprises
www.hempnut.bizland.com
Hemp seeds and oil products, hemp bath products, recipes forum, and history.

Govinda Foods
www.govinda-foods.com
All natural and original health foods. Maker of the Bliss Hemp Bar promoted by Ziggy Marley.

Santa Fe Hemp
www.santafehemp.com
Clothing, body care, handcrafted and natural products.

Indikah
www.indikah.com
Official site offering Indikah hempseed oil perfumes and colognes.

Canolio Cosmétiques
www.canolio.com
Natural hemp-based body-care line includes massage oil, foamy bath oil, soap, and moisturizing body milk. Online retail sales.

CHII of Canada
www.chii.ca
Supplies, facilitates, and diversifies the commercial hemp industry, while encouraging a 100 percent sustainable approach to all associated aspects. CHII is the source for the best possible quality organic hemp oil grown and processed in Canada.

Hemp in the Heartland
www.hemp-product.com
Sells a wide variety of hemp products—from stylish clothes made of hemp to pizza dough from hemp seeds.

The Merry Hempsters
www.merryhempsters.com/hemp_products.html
Hemp products for relief of chapped lips, sore muscles, cuts, abrasions, and bruises.

HempUtopia
www.canada-shops.com/stores/hemputopia
Industrial hemp retail store and information center. Hemp foods, body-care, books, paper, clothing, bags, and accessories.

BioHemp Technologies Ltd
www.biohemp.com
A Regina, Canada–based distributor of industrial hemp products including oil, flour, and seeds. Mum's Original certified organic hemp seed food products. Wholesale and retail.

Finola
www.finola.com
Producers of fine hempseed oil from Finland. Uses the FIN-314 Industrial Hemp variety.

Maine IntelliHemp Co.
www.intellihemp.com
Natural hemp products made in Maine, including lip balm, massage oil, and salve. Retail online ordering, and wholesale.

HempBed
www.hempbed.com
Highly absorbent industrial-hemp animal bedding from Kenex of Ontario, Canada.

DZined
www.dzinedonline.com
Uniquely hand-dyed knitting and weaving yarns in wool and wool/hemp blends, and wool/hemp spinning fibers from DZined.

Midwest Hemp
midwesthemp.bizhosting.com
Natural hemp clothing and accessories for the environmentally aware.

Hempart Cards
www.canada-shops.com/stores/jackdaw
Greeting cards depicting original art printed on fine hemp paper.

Healing Hemp
www.healinghemp.com
Certified organic hemp seed oil products for the mind, body, and soul. Also sells other hemp-related products.

Pacific Hemp
www.pacifichemp.com
Hempseed oil for nutritional, cosmetic, and industrial uses. Products include organic extra-virgin hemp oil (cold-pressed), virgin hemp oil (cold-pressed), and industrial grade (solvent extraction).

Fresh Hemp Foods Ltd.

www.freshhempfoods.com

Manitoba Harvest brand hemp foods. Online ordering, hemp field slide show, product descriptions, hemp seed nutrition facts, recipes, and FAQ.

American Hemp

www.ahbetterworld.com

American Hemp has the largest inventoried supply of hemp twine, cordage, rope, and webbing in the United States.

Crane Paper

www.crane.com/products/continuum/product-information-hemp.asp

Continuum Hemp paper is made with 50 percent hemp fiber and 50 percent recovered cotton rag, and is elemental chlorine-free.

EarthHemp.com

www.earthhemp.com

Only hemp products, including jeans, shorts, shirts, hats, bags, wallets, candles, shoes, toys, soaps, and hemp oil hot sauce. Online retail sales.

Sources

CHAPTER 1: ABOUT CANNABIS

P. 1 For a description of the botanical origins of hemp and its history as a religious and recreational drug, see Richard Evans Schultes and Albert Hoffman, *Plants of the Gods*. New York: McGraw Hill, 1979, p. 92–105.

For hemp history, see the long articles at globalhemp.com/Archives. Much of that material comes from the section on the History of the Medical Use of Marijuana, in The Report of the National Commission on Marihuana and Drug Abuse, *Marihuana: A Signal of Misunderstanding*, commissioned by President Richard M. Nixon, March, 1972. This study also has sections on early use of cannabis as a drug. See also Dr. Norman Taylor's "The Pleasant Assassin," in David Solomon (ed.), *The Marijuana Papers*. New York: Signet, 1966 p. 31–47.

See also the excellent material at Hempology.com and the Schaffer Drug Library at druglibrary.org/schaffer/hemp/history/first12000/abel.htm

Reefer Madness
Much of the historical material in this section is drawn from the historical sources used in chapter one.

P. 34 See *The Hasheesh Eater*, by Fitzhugh Ludlow, which was originally published anonymously. Parts of it are used in *The Marijuana Papers* (191–208).

P. 43 Description of the "tea pad" is from *The Marihuana Problem in The City of New York*, Mayor LaGuardia's Committee on Marijuana, submitted March 18, 1941.

P. 48 Sections on the debate on the *Marijuana Tax Stamp Act* of 1937 may be found on the globalhemp.com web site.

P. 51 Second Reading of Canada's *Narcotic Drug Act* (approval in principle) took place Feb. 24, 1935 and the text of the debate may be found in *House of Commons Debates*, 1938 (Vol. 1) p 772–79. See also *Fiber Wars: The Extinction of Kentucky Hemp*, by David P. West, Ph.D., published on the Internet at gametec.com/hemp/fiberwars/index.html. Gametec.com has other useful historical documents in its archives.

P. 54 Michigan Attorney General Raymond Starr's remarks were recorded by *The Globe and Mail*, July 16, 1938.

P. 58 See also "When Swat Raids Go Wrong," *The Capital Times* (Madison, WI), August 18, 2001.

P. 60 "Cops Bribe Hotel Workers" by Dana Larsen, *Cannabis Culture*, July, 1999.

P. 61 Celebrities and marijuana: Yahooka Hall of Fame (yahooka.com/halloffame.htm). See also "Reefer Madness," *Salon* Magazine, August 18, 1997.

CHAPTER 2: USES FOR CANNABIS

P. 71 Hempola has a web site, hempola.com. For other sources, see commercial web sites listed at the end of the book. See also Hemprecipes.com and Hemphasis.com, where the authors make the case for hemp protein.

P. 74 "Edible Hemp," *The Albuquerque Tribune*, March 12, 2002; and *Natural Health*, March/April 1993.

Fiber and Paper

P. 71 For papermaking, see hempunion.karoo.net/main/info/paper/book1.htm; artistictreasure.com/hemp_fortrees.html; hempfood.com/IHA/iha01105.html. See also H. Dewey and J.L. Merrill, "Hemp Hurds as Papermaking Material," *USDA Bulletin* No. 404, U.S. Government Printing Office, Washington, October 14, 1916; B. Parsad, et. al., "High-Kappa Pulping and Extended Oxygen Delignification Decreases Recovery Cycle Load" *TAPPI J.*, Vol. 77, No. 11, 1994, p. 135–147. For the report on switching Wisconsin's huge papermaking industry over to hemp, see gametec.com/hemp/mktanalysis.html.

Hemp: An Alternative Fuel

P. 81 See *Napa Valley Register*, March 15, 2002.

P. 82–86 Bill Kovarik, "Henry Ford, Charles Kettering and The Fuel of the Future," *Society of Automotive Historians*, 1998; "Ford Predicts Fuel from Vegetation," *New York Times*, September 20, 1925; Robert N. Tweedy, "Industrial Alcohol," 1954; Reynold Millard Wik, "Henry Ford's Science and Technology for Rural America," *Technology and Culture*, Summer, 1963.

P. 88 The ongoing story of the hemp car can be found at hempcar.org.

Medical Uses

Most of the material for this section comes from scientific journal articles listed below.

P. 93 See *High Times*, October 2002. See also *Therapeutic Hemp Oil*, by Andrew Weil, M.D.

P. 95 "Medical Marijuana: Annals of Internal Medicine and Perspectives Medicinal Applications of Delta-9-Tetrahydrocannabinol and Marijuana," *Annals of Internal Medicine* 15 May 1997. 126:791–98. Also extremely valuable is the special issue on marijuana, *New Scientist*, February 21, 1998, with a spirited pro and con debate.

P.96 "The Cannabis Remedy — Wonder Worker or Evil Weed?" *The Lancet*, December 20, 1997. See also "The Case for Marijuana Lights Up," *Globe and Mail*, May 11, 1991, p. D5.

P. 100 See U.S. Supreme Court Reports for *Conant v. McCaffrey* (1997) and *U.S. v. Oakland Cannabis Buyers Club* (2001).

P. 101 "DEA Raids Clinic," *Auburn Journal*, October 4, 2001. For the DEA's case against Dr. Fry, see U.S. Department of Justice Drug Enforcement Administration, Diversion Control Program, Registrant Actions, December 20, 2002.

P. 102 The Canadian media has given the Flin Flon project considerable coverage. See "Rock Tours Flin Flon Mine," *Globe and Mail*, June 3, 2002; "Government Ganja Mined in Flin Flon," *Winnipeg Sun*, May 1, 2003; "Sickly Group Battling for Medical Marijuana," *Winnipeg Sun*, May 1, 2003.

P. 103 "GW To Develop New Cannabinoid Opportunities with Professor Raphael Mechoulam," Press release issued by GW Pharmaceuticals, January 22, 2003.

CHAPTER 3: DEFYING THE DEA: THE FIGHT FOR CANNABIS

P. 106 For the story of Ken Hayes, see "Medical Pot Users Plead for Help," *The Press Democrat* (Santa Rosa, CA), June 16, 1999; also see articles at hempweed.com. For the DEA and hemp food issue, see "DEA Bans Hemp Products," *Chicago Tribune*, March 13, 2002.

P. 108 For articles on B.C. Bud, see "B.C. Bud, Vancouver's Cash Crop," *Vancouver Sun*, July 22, 2000; "Cannabis Cafe Offers Pot Smokers Tasteful

Menu High on Hemp Seeds," *Vancouver Sun*, June 24, 1997, p. B3; For the Drug Enforcement Administration's view of B.C. Bud, see "B.C. Bud: Growth of the Canadian Marijuana Trade," *Drug Enforcement Administration Intelligence Division*, December 2000; See also an interview with Neil Boyd, professor of sociology, Simon Fraser University, July, 2003.

P. 111 See *High Times*, Summer 2000, and *Cannabis Culture*, Summer 2000, for the ads.

P. 114 See Hempline's web site, hempline.com.

Decriminalization and Reaction

P. 118 For state action on hemp re-introduction, see "Legislation Affecting the Hemp Industry: Industrial Hemp Investigative and Advisory Task Force Approach," *Submitted to the Illinois House of Representatives*, January 26, 2000. This can be found on the Internet at www.thehia.org.

P. 119 "Canadian Producer Sues U.S. over Proposed DEA Hemp Ban," *Globe and Mail*, January 14, 2002.

P. 120 "Harrelson's Hemp Seeds Legal, Jury Says Quickly," *Lexington Herald Leader*, Kentucky, August 25, 2000.

P. 122 "Pro-hemp Teacher Fired; Schools Chief Cites Lying, Cheating." *ibid*, July 16, 1997.

P. 123 "DEA Stops Hemp Trade Cold," *Natural Food Merchandiser*, November, 1999. For Congressman Paul's article, see "Rock River," *Il Times*, September 19, 2001.

CHAPTER 4: GROWING YOUR OWN

There are several useful internet sites for people interested in cultivating cannabis. See overgrow.com; howtogrowmarijuana.com; and geocities.com/beginnerhelp2000. For an excellent guide to hydroponics, see Stewart Kenyon and M. Howard, *Hydroponics for the Home Gardner*. Toronto: Key Porter Books, 1992.

Bibliography

Books

Schultes, Richard Evans. *Plants of the Gods*. New York: McGraw Hill, 1979.

Solomon, David, ed. *The Marijuana Papers*. New York: Signet, 1966.

Zimmer, Lynn, and John P. Morgan. *Marijuana Myths, Marijuana Facts*. New York: The Lindesmith Center, 1997.

Journals and Periodicals

Annals of Internal Medicine. "Medicinal Uses of Marijuana." December 15, 1997.

The Atlantic. "Marijuana and the Law." September, 1994.

The Atlantic. "More Reefer Madness." April, 1997.

The Atlantic. "Reefer Madness." August, 1994.

British Medical Journal. "Cannabis as Medicine." Editorial, April 4, 1998.

British Medical Journal. "The War on Drugs." Editorial, December 23, 1995.

Chemistry and Industry. "Better Living Through Chemistry." January, 1998

Consumers Union of U.S., Inc. "Marijuana as Medicine." May, 1997.

The Denver Post. "War on Narcotics Imperils Justice System." November 2, 1997.

Dissent. "Chain Gang Blues." Fall 1996.

The Economist. "Campaign Issues: Drugs, All The President's Fault?" September 14, 1996.

The Economist. "Shopping for a Drugs Policy." August 16, 1997.

Foreign Affairs. "Commonsense Drug Policy." 77:1. January–February, 1998.

George. "Uncle Sam's Pot Farm." July, 1997.

Hotwired, The Netizen. "This Is Your Net On Drugs." June 27, 1997.

Journal of the American Medical Association: Medical News & Perspectives. "Lessons from U.S. History of Drug Use." June 25, 1997.

The Lancet. "The Cannabis Remedy—Wonder Worker or Evil Weed?" December 20, 1997.

The Lancet. "Deglamorising Cannabis." November 11, 1995.

The Lancet. "NIH Panel Debates Marijuana as Medicine." March 1, 1997.

The Lancet. "Why Britain's Drug Czar Mustn't Wage War on Drugs." Editorial by John Strang, August 9, 1997.

Liberty. "The Fight for Medical Marijuana." January, 1998.

Liberty. "Marijuana Sell-Out." March, 1997.

Liberty. "Smoke and Mirrors." Review, July, 1997.

The Nation. "The Battle For Medical Marijuana." January 6, 1997.

The Nation. "C.I.A., Crack, The Media." June 2, 1997.

The Nation. "Crack Reporting." November 18, 1996.

The Nation. "The Drug War's Hidden Economic Agenda." March 9, 1998.

The Nation. "The Drug War's Phony Fix. *Drug War Politics: The Price of Denial.*" April 28, 1997.

The Nation. "Legalizing Drugs: Just Say Yes." July 10, 1995.

The Nation. "The Phony Drug War." September 23, 1996.

The Nation. "Private Prisons." January 5, 1998.

The Nation. "War Ends, Drugs Win." January 6, 1997.

The Nation. "The War On Drugs Is Lost." February 12, 1996.

The Nation. "The Wrong Drug War." Editorial, March 23, 1998.

The National Review. "Abolish the Drug Laws?" July 1, 1996.

New England Journal of Medicine. "Federal Foolishness and Marijuana." January 30, 1997.

New England Journal of Medicine. "Marijuana, the Aids Wasting Syndrome, and the U.S. Government." September 7, 1995.

New England Journal of Medicine. "Reefer Madness—The Response to California's Medical Marijuana Law." August 7, 1997.

The New Republic. "Don't You D.A.R.E." March 3, 1997.

New Scientist. "A Dangerous Pathway." July 5, 1997.

New Scientist. "Chill Out, Man." June 21, 1997.

New Scientist. "Deadly Combination." July 12, 1997.

New Scientist. "Give a Drug a Bad Name..." April 6, 1996.

New Scientist. "Medical Marijuana Debate Moving Towards Closure." March 31, 1997.

New Scientist. "Press The Panic Button." January 25, 1997.

New Scientist. "Special Issue on Marijuana." February 21, 1998.

New Scientist. "Turn On, Tune In, Get Well." March 15, 1997.

New York Review of Books. "Drugs & the CIA." November 28, 1996.

Ottawa Citizen. "Decriminalizing Drugs: Four Editorials." April 12–16, 1997.

Playboy. "Time Out for Justice." December, 1997.

Reason. "Dazed and Confusing." August, 1996.

Reason. "Drug Prevention Placebo." March, 1995.

Reason. "Pot of Trouble." May, 1997.

Reason. "Prescription: Drugs." February, 1997.

Reason. "Reefer Madness." March, 1997.

Reason. "3 Books on Prohibition's Past and Present." Review, July, 1997.

Salon. "Reefer Madness." August 18, 1997.

Slate. "Do as We Say." April 19, 1997.

Slate. "I Smell a Rat." August 9, 1997.

Slate. "The New Politics of the Drug War." December 13, 1996.

Slate. "This Is Your Network on Drugs." March 15, 1997.

Times Literary Supplement. "Going Dutch: A Review of *Drugs, Crime and Corruption: Thinking the Unthinkable* by Richard Clutterbuck." Review by Edward N. Luttwak. September 1, 1995.

The Washington Monthly. "Why You Can Hate Drugs and Still Want to Legalize Them." October, 1995.

Wired News. "Taking on the Culture of Prohibition." July 3, 1997.

Xtra!. "Why Are the Media Enlisting in the Government's Crusade Against Marijuana?" July, 1997.

Acknowledgments

Thanks to Mike Mouland, ever-patient editor; Karen Rolfe, copy editor, who knows the full and quite limited range of my spelling skills; Clare McKeon and Janice Zawerbny at Key Porter; Daphne Hart; Gail Cohen and Michael Fitz-James at Canada Law Book; the brilliant and kind staff of the Library of Parliament; Fateema Sayani; Allan Rock; John Bell, Stu Lundy, and Dave LeBlanc; the co-operative and often quite eager people who helped source this book; my wife, who helped proof the galleys and my kids, who put up with my absences and were guinea pigs for various hemp products.

Index